DATE DUE

FEB 20 1995	
AUG 0 6 2011	

Modern Critical Interpretations

Stephen Crane's
The Red Badge of Courage

Modern Critical Interpretations

These and other titles in preparation

Modern Critical Interpretations

Stephen Crane's

The Red Badge of Courage

Edited and with an introduction by

Harold Bloom
Sterling Professor of the Humanities
Yale University

Chelsea House Publishers ◇ *1987*
NEW YORK ◇ NEW HAVEN ◇ PHILADELPHIA

Library of Congress Cataloging-in-Publication Data
Stephen Crane's The red badge of courage.
   (Modern critical interpretations)
   Bibliography: p.
   Includes index.
   Contents: The freedom of the poet / John Berryman—
Psychology and The red badge of courage / Daniel Weiss—
Order in The red badge of courage / Norman Lavers—
[etc.]
   1. Crane, Stephen, 1871–1900. Red badge of courage.
2. United States—History—Civil War, 1861–1865—
Literature and the war. I. Bloom, Harold. II. Series.
PS1449.C85R3976   1987   813'.4   86–20687
ISBN 1-55546-004-6 (alk. paper)

Contents

Editor's Note

This book brings together a representative selection of the best criticism devoted to Stephen Crane's masterly short novel, *The Red Badge of Courage*. The criticism is reprinted here in the chronological order of its original publication. I am grateful to Susan Laity, Frank Menchaca, and Peter Childers for their erudition and judgment in helping to edit this volume.

My introduction centers on Crane's originality in his representation of battle, with particular reference to the question of Crane's ironies. The chronological sequence begins with the poet John Berryman, who sees the *Red Badge* as a crucial transitional work between Tolstoy and Hemingway, two master visionaries of men at war. In his psychoanalytic reading, Daniel Weiss reads the fear of Henry Fleming against Ernest Hemingway's classic description of a "good soldier."

Norman Lavers, seeking an idea of order in the novel, finds in the book's imagery an implicit struggle for individuation. The important critical issue of literary impressionism in the *Red Badge* is addressed by James Nagel, for whom "the drama of the novel is epistemological, a matter of perception, distortion, and realization." Harold Beaver's reading endows the familiar critical trope of "the hero as victim" with the pathos of "nervous integrity" and of a pre-Hemingway code of self-possession.

The book concludes with three innovative recent reappraisals. Donald Pease, considering the book as a war narrative, argues that in the *Red Badge*, "narratives do not follow battles and provide needed explanation; instead, they precede and indeed demand battles as elaborations and justifications of already narrated events." Henry Fleming's battle-fury is studied by Chester L. Wolford in the context of Crane's preternatural control of the epic mode of the agonistic, of the contest of consciousness that takes place between the writers of this tradition.

In the final essay of this book, Michael Fried explores the fascinating analogues between the work of the painter Eakins and Crane's novel, since each equates artistic representation with processes of disfiguration. Fried fittingly ends this book by providing a refreshingly different perspective on the *Red Badge*, a perspective that is likely to be prophetic of much future criticism of Crane's masterpiece.

Introduction

Stephen Crane's contribution to the canon of American literature is fairly slight in bulk: one classic short novel, three vivid stories, and two or three ironic lyrics. *The Red Badge of Courage*; "The Open Boat," "The Blue Hotel," and "The Bride Comes to Yellow Sky"; "War is Kind" and "A Man Adrift on a Slim Spar" —a single small volume can hold them all. Crane was dead at twenty-eight, after a frantic life, but a longer existence probably would not have enhanced his achievement. He was an exemplary American writer, flaring in the forehead of the morning sky and vanishing in the high noon of our evening land. An original, if not quite a Great Original, he prophesied Hemingway and our other journalist-novelists and still seems a forerunner of much to come.

The Red Badge of Courage is Crane's undoubted masterwork. Each time I reread it, I am surprised afresh, particularly by the book's originality, which requires a reader's act of recovery because Crane's novel has been so influential. To write about battle in English, since Crane, is to be shadowed by Crane. Yet Crane, who later saw warfare in Cuba and between the Greeks and the Turks in his work as a correspondent, had experienced no fighting when he wrote *The Red Badge of Courage.* There is no actual experience that informs Crane's version of the Battle of Chancellorsville, one of the most terrible carnages of the American Civil War. Yet anyone who has gone through warfare, from the time of the novel's publication (1895) until now, has testified to Crane's uncanny accuracy at the representation of battle. *The Red Badge of Courage* is an impressionist's triumph, in the particular sense that "impressionist" had in the literature of the nineties, a Paterian sense that went back to the emphasis upon *seeing* in Carlyle, Emerson,

1

and Ruskin. Conrad and Henry James, both of whom befriended Crane, had their own relation to the impressionist mode, and each realized that Crane was a pure or natural impressionist, indeed the only one, according to Conrad.

Pater, deftly countering Matthew Arnold, stated the credo of literary impressionism:

> The first step towards seeing one's object as it really is, is
> to know one's impression as it really is, to discriminate it,
> to realize it distinctly.

Pater's "object" is a work of art, verbal or visual, but the critic here has stated Stephen Crane's quest to see the object of experience as it is, to know one's impression of it, and to realize that impression in narrative fiction. Scholarly arguments as to whether and to what degree *The Red Badge of Courage* is naturalistic, symbolist, or impressionist, can be set aside quickly. Joyce's *Ulysses* is both naturalistic and symbolist within the general perspective of the Paterian or impressionistic "epiphany" or privileged moment, but juxtapose the *Red Badge* to *Ulysses* and Crane is scarcely naturalistic or symbolist in comparison. Crane is altogether an impressionist, in his "vivid impressionistic description of action on that woodland battlefield," as Conrad phrased it, or, again in Conrad's wording, in "the imaginative analysis of his own temperament tried by the emotions of a battlefield."

If Crane's impressionism had a single literary origin, as to some extent is almost inevitable, Kipling is that likely forerunner. The puzzles of literary ancestry are most ironical here, since Kipling's precursor was Mark Twain. Hemingway's famous observation that all modern American literature comes out of one book, *Huckleberry Finn*, is only true of Crane, the indubitable beginning of our modern literature, insofar as Crane took from Kipling precisely what the author of *The Light That Failed* and *Kim* owed to Twain. Michael Fried's association of Crane with the painter Eakins is peculiarly persuasive, since Crane's visual impressionism is so oddly American, without much resembling Whistler's. Crane is almost the archetype of the writer as a child of experience, yet I think this tends to mean that then there are a few strong artistic precursors, rather than a tradition that makes itself available. Associate Crane with Kipling and Eakins, on the way to, but still a distance from, Conrad and the French Postimpressionists, and you probably have stationed him accurately enough.

II

The Red Badge of Courage is necessarily a story about fear. Crane's Young Soldier, again as Conrad noted, "dreads not danger but fear itself. . . . In this he stands for the symbol of all untried men." Henry Fleming, as eventually we come to know the Young Soldier, moves ironically from a dangerous self-doubt to what may be an even more dangerous dignity. This is the novel's famous yet perhaps equivocal conclusion:

> For a time this pursuing recollection of the tattered man took all elation from the youth's veins. He saw his vivid error, and he was afraid that it would stand before him all his life. He took no share in the chatter of his comrades, nor did he look at them or know them, save when he felt sudden suspicion that they were seeing his thoughts and scrutinizing each detail of the scene with the tattered soldier.
>
> Yet gradually he mustered force to put the sin at a distance. And at last his eyes seemed to open to some new ways. He found that he could look back upon the brass and bombast of his earlier gospels and see them truly. He was gleeful when he discovered that he now despised them.
>
> With this conviction came a store of assurance. He felt a quiet manhood, nonassertive but of sturdy and strong blood. He knew that he would no more quail before his guides wherever they should point. He had been to touch the great death, and found that, after all, it was but the great death. He was a man.
>
> So it came to pass that as he trudged from the place of blood and wrath his soul changed. He came from hot plowshares to prospects of clover tranquilly, and it was as if hot plowshares were not. Scars faded as flowers.
>
> It rained. The procession of weary soldiers became a bedraggled train, despondent and muttering, marching with churning effort in a trough of liquid brown mud under a low, wretched sky. Yet the youth smiled, for he saw that the world was a world for him, though many discovered it to be made of oaths and walking sticks. He had rid himself of the red sickness of battle. The sultry nightmare was in the past. He had been an animal blistered and sweating in the heat and pain of war. He turned now with a lover's

thirst to images of tranquil skies, fresh meadows, cool brooks—an existence of soft and eternal peace.

Over the river a golden ray of sun came through the hosts of leaden rain clouds.

More Hemingway than Hemingway are these very American sentences: "He had been to touch the great death, and found that, after all, it was but the great death. He was a man." Is the irony of that dialectical enough to suffice? In context, the power of the irony is beyond question, since Crane's prose is strong enough to bear rephrasing as: "He had been to touch the great fear, and found that, after all, it was still the great fear. He was not yet a man." Crane's saving nuance is that the fear of being afraid dehumanizes, while accepting one's own mortality bestows upon one the association with others that grants the dignity of the human. How does Crane's prose find the strength to sustain a vision that primary and normative? The answer, I suspect, is the Bible and Bunyan, both of them being deeply at work in this unbelieving son of a Methodist minister: "He came from hot plowshares to prospects of clover tranquilly, and it was as if hot plowshares were not." The great trope of Isaiah is assimilated in the homely and unassuming manner of Bunyan, and we see the Young Soldier, Henry Fleming, as an American Pilgrim, anticipating when both sides of the Civil War "shall beat their swords into plowshares, and their spears into pruning hooks."

III

Crane's accurate apprehension of the phantasmagoria that is battle has been compared to Tolstoy's. There is something to such a parallel, perhaps because Tolstoy even more massively is a biblical writer. What is uniquely Crane's, what parts him from all prior visionaries of warfare, is difficult to define, but is of the highest importance for establishing his astonishing originality. Many examples might be chosen, but I give the death of the color sergeant from the conclusion of chapter 19:

> Over the field went the scurrying mass. It was a handful of men splattered into the faces of the enemy. Toward it instantly sprang the yellow tongues. A vast quantity of blue smoke hung before them. A mighty banging made ears valueless.
>
> The youth ran like a madman to reach the woods before a bullet could discover him. He ducked his head low, like

a football player. In his haste his eyes almost closed, and the scene was a wild blur. Pulsating saliva stood at the corners of his mouth.

Within him, as he hurled himself forward, was born a love, a despairing fondness for this flag which was near him. It was a creation of beauty and invulnerability. It was a goddess, radiant, that bended its form with an imperious gesture to him. It was a woman, red and white, hating and loving, that called him with the voice of his hopes. Because no harm could come to it he endowed it with power. He kept near, as if it could be a saver of lives, and an imploring cry went from his mind.

In the mad scramble he was aware that the color sergeant flinched suddenly, as if struck by a bludgeon. He faltered, and then became motionless, save for his quivering knees.

He made a spring and a clutch at the pole. At the same instant his friend grabbed it from the other side. They jerked at it, stout and furious, but the color sergeant was dead, and the corpse would not relinquish its trust. For a moment there was a grim encounter. The dead man, swinging with bended back, seemed to be obstinately tugging, in ludicrous and awful ways, for the possession of the flag.

It was past in an instant of time. They wrenched the flag furiously from the dead man, and, as they turned again, the corpse swayed forward with bowed head. One arm swung high, and the curved hand fell with heavy protest on the friend's unheeding shoulder.

In the "wild blur" of this phantasmagoria, there are two images of pathos, the flag and the corpse of the color sergeant. Are they not to some degree assimilated to one another, so that the corpse becomes a flagpole, and the flag a corpse? Yet so dialectical is the interplay of Crane's biblical irony that the assimilation, however incomplete, itself constitutes a figure of doubt as to the normative intensities of patriotism and group solidarity that the scene exemplifies, both in the consciousness of Henry Fleming and in that of the rapt reader. The "despairing fondness" for the flag is both a Platonic and a Freudian Eros, but finally more Freudian. It possesses "invulnerability" for which the soldier under fire has that Platonic desire for what he himself does not possess and quite desperately needs, but it manifests even more a Freudian sense of the ambivalence both of and towards the woman as object of the drive, at once a radiant goddess sexually bending her form though imperiously, yet also a woman, red and white, hating and loving, destroying and healing.

The corpse of the color sergeant, an emblem of devotion to the flag and the group even beyond death, nevertheless keeps Fleming and his friend from the possibility of survival as men, compelling them to clutch and jerk at the pole, stout and furious. Life-in-death incarnate, the corpse obstinately tugs for the staff of its lost life. Homer surely would have appreciated the extraordinary closing gesture, as the corpse sways forward, head bowed but arm swung high for a final stroke, as "the curved hand fell with heavy protest on the friend's unheeding shoulder."

Crane is hardly the American Homer; Walt Whitman occupies that place forever. Still, *The Red Badge of Courage* is certainly the most Homeric prose narrative ever written by an American. One wants to salute it with Whitman's most Homeric trope, when he says of the grass:

And now it seems to me the beautiful uncut hair of graves.

The Freedom of the Poet

John Berryman

The wars of men have inspired the production of some of man's chief works of art, but very undemocratically. Napoleon's wars inspired Goya, Stendhal, Beethoven, Tolstoy; a prolonged bicker of 1100 B.C. inspired the poet of the *Iliad,* who celebrated and deplored three centuries later a little piece of it near its end; the Wars of the Roses resulted in Shakespeare's giant effort, again long afterward; the Athenian empire's ruin was adequately dramatized by a participant, the greatest of historians; Picasso made something of the soul-destroying civil war in his native country. But what came of Cromwell's war? Or of the atrocious conflict between North and South in the United States?— thirty years after it ended came a small novel by a very young man called *The Red Badge of Courage.* The immediate literature of the Civil War has been beautifully studied of late in Edmund Wilson's *Patriotic Gore,* but no one, I think, would claim for that literature any such eminence as belongs, after now almost seventy years, to Stephen Crane's novel. A critic seems to be faced, then, with alternative temptations: to overrate it, as an American, because it chronicles our crucial struggle, or to underrate it, in the grand perspective of the artists just mentioned, because it appears to assert neither the authority of the experienced warrior nor the authority of the historical artist—Tolstoy having both, Thucydides both. Crane was no scholar and had seen no battle. Yet some authority has got to be allowed him, and identified, for his work has not only brilliantly survived but was recognized

From *The Freedom of the Poet.* © 1965 by Basic Books. Farrar, Straus & Giroux, 1976.

instantly abroad—in England—as authentic; professional military men were surprised to learn that he was not one.

It is hard to see how anyone, except a casual reader, could over-rate *The Red Badge of Courage* for patriotic reasons, because, though the book does indeed handle parts of the battle of Chancellorsville, it is not really about the Civil War. For instance, it shows no interest in the causes, meaning, or outcome of the war; no interest in politics; no interest in tactics or strategy. In this book, these failures are a merit, in opposition to the supreme fault of *War and Peace,* which is philosophical and programmatic. Here we have only parts of one minor battle, seen from one ignorant point of view, that of a new volunteer. One would never guess that what has been called the first modern war was being studied. All the same, as from the weird diagrams of Samuel Beckett, the helpless horror of modern man emerges: we learn, as we learn from few books, about the waiting, the incomprehension, rumour, frustration, anxiety, fatigue, panic, hatred not only of the enemy but of officers; about complaints of "bad luck" and the sense of betrayal by commanders. This is a losing army. Since every intelligent man has to be at some point afraid of proving himself a coward—which is what the ordeal of Crane's protagonist is about—the story presents itself to us initially as making some claim to universality; and the claim is strengthened by Crane's reluctance to divulge the name of the hero (it is Henry Fleming) or the names of the only other two people who matter—the tall soldier (Jim) and the loud youth (Wilson)—or the iden-tity of the regiment, or the geography. By *leaving things out* the author makes his general bid for our trust.

But of course he has put in things, too, and our problems are where he got them and how he put them. The main things he put in are: reflection and action. Much of the book really is battle. Crane had read *Sevastopol,* Tolstoy's short novel, and declared that he learned what war was like from football—after starring in baseball at the two colleges he briefly attended, he coached a boys' football team in New Jersey. One of the staff at his military academy, a major-general, had seen ac-tion at Chancellorsville and liked to talk about it. Crane had played war games as a child, and talked with veterans, and read (with disap-pointment and contempt) magazine articles on the war. Later, after witnessing substantial parts of the Greco-Turkish War, he said, *"The Red Badge* is all right." I don't know that we can say precisely how he learned what he knew, except to recognize in him an acute visual imagination and an inspired instinct for what happens and what does not happen in conflict. Here is a short passage:

> He expected a battle scene.
> There were some little fields girted and squeezed by a forest. Spread over the grass and in among the tree trunks, he could see knots and waving lines of skirmishers who were running hither and thither and firing at the landscape. A dark battle line lay upon a sunstruck clearing that gleamed orange color. A flag fluttered.
> Other regiments floundered up the bank.

Some of the features of Crane's *style* appear: his convulsive and also humourous irony ("expected," as if he would not see it but he saw it, and "firing at the landscape"), its violent animism ("squeezed"), its descriptive energy ("knots and waving lines" —like an abstract expressionist painting). But a Tolstoyan sense also of futility and incomprehension is swiftly conveyed, and this is only partly a product of style. He is inventing, he is experimenting. Crane himself goes in for this language—he several times speaks of "experiment" and says of the youth, "He tried to mathematically prove to himself that he would not run from a battle." In the action, then, the fantastic and the literal cooperate. The reflective aspects of the novel are another matter.

The scene of this extremely simple novel is laid in a single mind. It starts with soldiers speculating loudly about whether there is going to be a fight or not. Then "a youthful private" goes off to his hut: "He wished to be alone with some new thoughts that had lately come to him." This has the effect of understatement, putting so flatly the youth's debate with himself about his honour, but it is literal, besides introducing the theme of intense isolation that dominated Crane's work until the later story, his masterpiece, "The Open Boat," where human cooperation in face of the indifference of nature is the slowly arrived-at subject. Here his youth broods in private, having crawled into his dilemma, or hut, "through an intricate hole that served it as a door" —and the rest of the book provides a workout of the plight. On the first day he does well, and then runs away. A Union soldier clubs him in the panic retreat; Crane's ironic title refers to the "badge" of that wound; the youth is taken for a good soldier. He witnesses the death of his boyhood friend, the tall soldier, a true hero. Returned, by the kindness of a stranger to his regiment, he is cared for as a combatant by the loud youth—toward whom he is also enabled to feel superior in that, scared, earlier, Wilson entrusted him with letters to be sent in the event of his death and has now, shamefacedly, to ask for them back. Next day he fights like a hero or a demon. Such is the story. Perhaps many readers take it as a novel of development, a sort of success story, and this view is encouraged by the climactic passage: "He felt a quiet manhood, non-assertive but of sturdy and strong blood. . . . He had been to touch the great death, and found that, after all, it was but the great death. He was a man," and so on.

It is possible to feel very uncomfortable with this way of looking at the book.

For one thing, pervasive irony is directed toward the youth—his self-importance, his self-pity, his self-loving war rage. For another, we have only one final semi-self-reproach for his cowardice and imposture: "He saw that he was good. . . . Nevertheless, the ghost of his flight from the first engagement appeared to him and danced. There were small shoutings in his brain about these matters. For a moment he blushed, and the light of his soul flickered with shame." I find it hard to believe that Crane is here exonerating his hero, without irony. Finally, we have very early on an indication of his pomposity (his mother's "I know how you are, Henry"), and there is pomposity in his opinion of himself as a war demon. That would suggest a circular action, in the coward middle of which he appeared to reveal his real nature, or in fact did reveal it, by running. The irony embraces, then, all but the central failure.

It is easy to feel uncomfortable with his view, too—the more particularly because the apparent wound of the first day is indeed a real wound, and its silent pretension is later justified. On the other hand. . . . The irony never ends. I do not know what Crane intended. Probably he intended to have his cake and eat it, too—irony to the end, but heroism, too. Fair enough. How far did he fail?

Again I invoke, as praiseworthy, that which is not done. The youth is frantically afraid of being found out (he never is found out), but except in the passage just quoted, he never suffers the remorse one would expect. Intimate as Crane is with his hero psychologically, still the view he takes of him is cold, unsentimental, remote. This certainly preserves him from any full failure (though there have been many good readers from the day the book was published to now who have not liked it, because they regarded it as artificial and sensational).

The coldness leads to a certain impersonality, and it is a very striking fact that some of Crane's deepest private interests find no place in the novel—are deliberately excluded. Three of these are worth singling out. In his earlier novel, or long story, called *Maggie,* laid in New York's Bowery, Crane dramatized a distinct social philosophy—environmentalist, deterministic, and convinced that "the root of slum-life" was "a sort of cowardice." Yet his indifference to society in *The Red Badge* is complete, and it will not do here to say, "Of course it would be," for an army *is* society.

So with the matter of personal philosophy. We happen to know Crane's views perfectly, because he put them at length in letters to a girl (Nellie Crouse) by whom he was fascinated in 1895–96. We have time for a passage: "For my own part, I am minded to die in my thirty-fifth year [he died at twenty-eight, in 1900]. I think that is all I care to stand. I don't like to make wise remarks on the aspect of life but I will say that it doesn't strike me as particularly worth the trouble. The final wall of the wise man's thought however is Human Kindness of course"—and, exceptionally for him, Crane capitalized the two words. Now it might have been supposed that, bringing his hero through to maturity in *The Red Badge,* he would have got down to work in this area. But no. It seems impossible not to conclude that the splendid burst of rhetoric with which the novel concludes is just that, *in part*—a burst of rhetoric—and that Crane retained many of his reservations about his hero. As the wisest of modern British novelists, E. M. Forster, once observed, novels almost never end well—character desires to keep on going, whereas remorseless plot requires it to end. I hardly remember a better instance. Yet the last page is confidently and brilliantly done:

> It rained. The procession of weary soldiers became a bedraggled train, despondent and muttering, marching with churning effort in a trough of liquid brown mud under a low, wretched sky. Yet the youth smiled, for he saw that the world was a world for him, though many discovered it to be made of oaths and walking sticks. He had rid himself of the red sickness of battle.

But *then* comes a sentence in which I simply do not believe: "He turned now with a lover's thirst to images of tranquil skies, fresh meadows, cool brooks—an existence of soft and eternal peace." In short, we are left after all with a *fool,* for Crane knew as well as the next man, and much better, that life consists of very little but struggle. He wrote to Miss Crouse of "a life of labor and sorrow. I do not confront it blithely. I confront it with desperate resolution. There is not even much hope in my attitude. [Perhaps I may mention that at this point Stephen Crane was an international celebrity.] I do not even expect to do good. But I expect to make a sincere, desperate, lonely battle to remain true to my conception of my life and the way it should be lived. . . . It is not a fine prospect." The shutting out of his hero from his personal thought redeems for me, on the whole, the end of the book.

The absence of interest in religion in *The Red Badge of Courage* is more surprising still than the other indifferences, whether seen in a critical way or in a biographical way. Henry Fleming, orphan of a farm widow, was seminary-trained. What emerges from the training is scanty indeed. "He would die; he would go to some place where he would be understood. It was useless to expect appreciation of his profound and fine sense from such men as the lieutenant." This is a fine and funny passage, not deeply Christian. Then there's the famous passage about the wafer, long quoted as a war cry for modernism in American fictional art. Unutterably wounded, upright, the tall soldier had sought a private ground away from the retreat, in a field mysteriously chosen, followed by the youth and a tattered soldier, for his dance of death.

> As the flap of the blue jacket fell away from the body, he could see that the side looked as if it had been chewed by wolves.
>
> The youth turned, with sudden, livid rage, toward the battlefield. He shook his fist. He seemed about to deliver a philippic.
>
> "Hell—"
>
> The red sun was pasted in the sky like a wafer.

Pasting is a failingly temporary operation, I suppose—for the pagan god of the sky?!—handed us here as an overpowering rebuke to the youth's rebellion. A wafer is thick nourishment, too, is it not? Disdain and fury against the prerogatives of majesty seem to be the subject. But I notice two points. Even here it is hard to decide just how far Crane is with the youth and how far critical of him. And revolt, in a seminary youth, should have been better prepared: one would welcome a *trace* of his Christian history, pro or con; what Crane never provides. Shortly afterward we hear: "He searched about in his mind for an adequate malediction for the indefinite cause, the thing upon which men turn the words of final blame. It—whatever it was—was responsible for him, he said. There lay the fault."

Crane did not here believe in evil. Henry Fleming is not evil, nor is anyone. A strange setup for an ambitious novel. Determinism is in control ("It ... was responsible for him") or is it? for the next little words are *"he said"* —which may be a repudiation. Again we are in the seesaw.

It is not a bad place to be, so long as one trusts the writer.

Crane's religious history I'll do briefly. He could not help being the son of a clergyman and of a madly missionary woman: "that cooled off [he told an interviewer] and when I was thirteen or about that, my brother Will told me not to believe in Hell after my uncle had been boring me about the lake of fire and the rest of the side-shows." "I cannot be shown [he said at another time] that God bends upon us any definable stare, and his laughter would be bully to hear out in nothingness." I think we may conclude that neither this personal opinion nor the fierce scorn of Christianity that flashes in many of Crane's brilliant poems has anything really to do with the purely naturalistic framework—from this point of view—of *The Red Badge of Courage*.

With the word "naturalistic," however, we turn to some consideration of the artistic affiliations of the novel. All the categorical terms that have been applied to Crane's art are slippery, but let me deny at once that he was a Naturalist. The Naturalists—Frank Norris, say, and Theodore Dreiser—are accumulative and ponderous. Crane's intense selectivity makes him almost utterly unlike them. Crane himself, when hardly more than a boy, allied his creed to the Realism preached—in revolt against the slack, contrived, squeamish standards of popular American fiction in the nineties—by his first admirers, William Dean Howells, then the country's leading critic, and a younger writer, Hamlin Garland. But Crane's work does not resemble theirs, either, and he seems to have meant, in his alliance, only that art should be "sincere" (one of his favorite words) and truthful. Like many another young genius, he regarded most writers as frauds and liars—and, in fact, perhaps most writers *are* frauds and liars. But epithets so vague as "sincere" and "truthful" tell us very little. The best term is undoubtedly that of his close friend, the far greater novelist Joseph Conrad (though whether a *better* writer it is probably too soon to say), who observed in a letter to a mutual friend that "He is *the* only impressionist, and *only* an impressionist."

If we can accept this characteristically exaggerated but authoritative judgment, we are in a position to make some reservations. Conrad and Crane, when they met in England in 1897, recognized immediately an affinity; Conrad was soon charged by reviewers with imitating Crane (a charge he denied to Crane), and in truth parts of *Lord Jim* are much indebted to *The Red Badge;* yet Conrad clearly did not regard himself as an impressionist. Next, there exist in Crane's work obviously realistic and fantastic elements—as in Conrad's and in their friend Henry James's, also domiciled in the south of England at this time—two Americans and a Pole recreating English fiction, which was languishing, so far as form was concerned, in the powerful hands of Thomas Hardy and Rudyard Kipling. The power of *experiment* came from abroad, as later from Joyce and Hemingway and Kafka—and in poetry from T. S. Eliot and Ezra Pound.

Finally, his use of irony enters so deeply into most of Crane's finest work—all the five last authors named are ironists—that the simple term "impressionist" will hardly do, and my uncertain feeling is that Crane is best thought of as a twentieth-century author. Authorities date modern American literature, some from *The Red Badge* in 1895, some from the reissue the following year of *Maggie.* This is no occasion for an exposition of the nature of irony, in relation to Crane—which in any case I have attempted elsewhere—but maybe something of that will emerge from a summary study of his style. By way, though, of winding up the impressionist reservations, let me enforce Conrad's label with a quotation from Crane: "I understand that a man is born into the world with his own pair of eyes and he is not at all responsible for his vision—he is merely responsible for his quality of personal honesty. To keep close to this personal honesty is my supreme ambition." Ill, dying indeed, hard-pressed with guests and fame and need for money, working incessantly, he said to a journalist visitor during his last year of life: "I get a little tired of saying, Is this true?" He was an impressionist: he dealt in the way things strike one—but also in the way things are.

This famous style is not easy to describe, combining as it does characteristics commonly antithetical. It is swift, no style in English more so, improvisatorial, manly as Hazlitt; but at the same time it goes in for ritual solemnity and can be highly poetic. I illustrate. For speed: "For a moment he felt in the face of his great trial like a babe, and the flesh over his heart seemed very thin. He seized time to look about him calculatingly." Here we are already into something like the other category, illustrated in the opening sentence of the novel: "The cold passed reluctantly from the earth, and the retiring fogs revealed an army stretched out on the hills, resting." Here's a high case of the animism I have referred to. The colour of the style is celebrated—maybe he got it from a theory of Goethe's; but the style is also plain. Short as it is, it is also unusually iterative; modern and simple, brazen with medieval imagery; animistic, de-human and mechanistic; attentive—brilliantly—to sound: "As he ran, he became aware that the forest had stopped its music, as if at last becoming capable of hearing the foreign sounds. The trees hushed and stood motionless. Everything seemed to be listening to the crackle and clatter and ear-shaking thunder. The chorus pealed over the still earth." Adverbs are used like verbs, word order deformed: somebody leans on a bar and hears other men "terribly discuss a question that was not plain." But the surest attribute of this style is its reserve, as its most celebrated is its colour. Crane guarantees nothing. "Doubtless" is a favorite word. The technique of refusal is brought so far forward that a casual "often" will defeat itself: "What hats and caps were left to them they often slung high in the air." Once more we hear a Shakespearean contempt, as in *Coriolanus*. In a paradoxical way: if he won't vouch for what he tells us—if he doesn't push us, trying to convince—he must have things up his sleeve which if we knew them would persuade us. As for colour: "A crimson roar came from the distance" —the mildest example I have been able to find. His employment of it here is not only not naturalistic—what roar was ever red?—but is solely affective, that is, emotional; like his metaphorical use, in the novel, of devils, ghouls, demons, spectres. Crane made use of a spectrum. A final item is his rueful humour: "He threw aside his mental pamphlets on the philosophy of the retreated and rules for the guidance of the damned."

On that note we might end, except for a poem written by Stephen Crane several years after the novel called "War Is Kind," one of his major poems, and one of the best poems of the period in the United States of America.

In the novel there is little of the pathos of which he had already shown himself a master in *Maggie,* and little of the horror informing his best later war stories. They come to life in the poem. Crane makes a sort of little bridge between Tolstoy—supreme—supreme?—and our very good writer Hemingway. But these superior gentlemen do not compete. One of the best remarks ever made about the poet of the *Iliad* is that he shared with Tolstoy and with Shakespeare both a virile love of war and a virile horror of it. So in his degree did Crane, and before he had seen it.

Psychology and *The Red Badge of Courage*

Daniel Weiss

The psychoanalyst W. H. Frink writes about the emotions: "An emotion, one might say, is an undischarged action, a deed yet retained within the organism. Thus anger is unfought combat; fear unfled flight. Perhaps it would be more accurate to say that an emotion is a state of preparedness for action, which, however, in many ways is almost action itself."

What is perenially impressive about *The Red Badge of Courage* is its innerness of experience, comparable in its handling of developmental changes to the subjective ordeals of Richard Feverel and Stephen Dedalus. It is an epic imitation of an emotion rather than of an action, and so becomes, as Frink suggests, another form and, I suggest, perhaps a more intense form, of action. Crane's veracity is less a matter of reconstructing a historical event which may have accompanied it. As we shall see, Crane's grasp of the sense of fear did not change when he found his war, and *his* profoundest study of terror, "The Blue Hotel," has nothing military about it. Crane's success lies in his having achieved the crystalline essence of the emotion he set out to describe.

We may begin by generalizing on the situation in which Henry Fleming finds himself. He is a part of a social group that is confronted as a group with some palpable threat of physical danger. To men who are for the first time in such a situation, the normal anxieties are predictably twofold: the first is the anxious anticipation of physical danger and possible destruction—a personal, intrapsychic anxiety; the second

From *The Critic Agonistes: Psychology, Myth, and the Art of Fiction,* edited by Eric Solomon and Stephen Arkin. © 1985 by the University of Washington Press.

17

is outwardly directed, a matter of relationship, a social concern, involving one's self-esteem and loyalty to the small group in which one serves. Such a situation proposes an immediate challenge to how well the individual has formulated his sense of himself, and the modifications that attend his response to such pressures are an index to the quality and strength of this formulation.

Fleming's tender youth, as we might expect, precludes his achieving the serenity of his friend Jim Conklin. He is, we might say, the delicate neophyte, carefully chosen for precisely those qualities he is most deficient in, and for the one quality, "that craven scruple of thinking too precisely on th' event," that will make his initiation an affair of some moment rather than a casual transition. Literature is, of course, full of Henry Flemings. One thinks immediately of Conrad's captain in "The Secret Sharer," wondering as he stands his quixotic anchor watch, "how far I should turn out faithful to that ideal conception of one's own personality every man sets up for himself secretly." As for the others (and the captain's thought gives the lie to "every man"), "they had simply to be equal to their tasks." So Henry Fleming, at the first intimations of battle, feels himself an "unknown quantity," and begins immediately to look for himself, "continually trying to measure himself by his comrades, looking for kindred emotions," yet at the same time with the baffling sense of alienation, the sense of being "separated from the others."

Berryman comments brilliantly and definitively on the introspective candor of Crane's characters, their Hamlet-like awareness of the polarities of seeming and being. "There is regularly," he writes, "an element of pathos, therefore, in his ironic (oppositional) inspection, and an element of irony regularly in his pathos. A Crane creation or character normally is *pretentious* and *scared*—the human condition; fitted by the second for pathos, by the first for irony. If the second feeling can save the first, as in Henry Fleming, the first can doom the second, as in the Swede (in 'The Blue Hotel')."

Henry Fleming's search for some standard by which to measure himself, his "ideal conception," settles itself on the "tall soldier," who is, even after he dies, oracular to Henry's expectations, anxieties, and hopes. Yet we must anticipate that Jim Conklin's reassurances are finally false reassurances, the identification which is only the penultimate step toward identity. Claims of pretension and fear, to use Berryman's counters, must give way to some more viable position.

Heroes in literature are, as I have suggested, heavily endowed with a faculty for self-concern, to which we may add those handmaidens to intelligence, the faculties of interest and curiosity. Henry Fleming is so endowed; it is his major differentia. Interest and curiosity are ill-suited to the life of action in almost the same degree that they are well-suited to the learning process. They are onlookers' faculties, passive, receptive, requiring always a safe distance between subject and object. To the interested and the curious the wholesome state of preparedness for danger is lacking, and any untoward activity on the part of the observed object leads to terror, flight, and with it a radical loss of interest. Henry Fleming's interest and curiosity are the elements which attracted him to the war, for he sees it as an anachronistic survival, and in his fantasies he goes into battle as if he were going into a museum of antiquities. War is a matter of the past, a "Greek-like struggle," a Homeric fantasy. "Men were better or more timid. Secular and religious education had effaced the throat-grappling instinct." He has, in other words, set up an aesthetic and historical distance, a strategy of denial, between himself and the actuality. He has not yet left the classroom.

Crane, we may observe here, elects at all times, for his soldiers, this role of spectator in the presence of hostile *objects*. In his battles the agents of death—weapons, a tangible enemy, the errors and coups of strategists—become a negligible aspect in the individual's struggles to master his anxieties. Henry Fleming's first successful stand against the enemy is not a stand against anything. His interest and curiosity, when they are challenged by the resistance of the "phantom" enemy, result not in anxiety, which is a state of preparedness, but in panic, which is an intolerable excess of unanticipated emotion.

This, then, is the hero that Crane sends into battle. The hero's response to danger, like that of his comrades in arms, will have been conditioned from childhood into patterns of defense and aggression, whose strength and weaknesses will be found out under stress. He will, like his comrades, face a limited number of more or less determinate alternatives of response; a psychological naturalism will assert itself, less subject to the options of consciousness, because levels of mind and experience archaic to the uses of mature and peaceable culture are being invoked exclusively. The restrictions of Henry Fleming's point of view, his personal response, would do Henry James credit.

We must, let me assert parenthetically, rule out one alternative response, the one most associated with war and calamity, the fully developed traumatic neurosis. In such cases, better suited to clinical than to literary description, all adaptations to the world and all the higher motor and mental functions are swept under in the psychological debacle of trauma. We are dealing in Crane's novel with adaptations that are familiar to us, by which men under pressure maintain their equilibrium both within themselves and in relation to the world of friends and foes, of dangers and refuges from danger. The simplified, monothematic conditions under which Henry Fleming operates give these adaptations a greater clarity than they would possess under other conditions.

The overall motif in *The Red Badge of Courage* is Henry Fleming's obsessive need to purge himself of fear. The novel is in psychological terms a study of anxiety-defense mechanisms working under pressure to establish some tolerable adaptation to a dangerous reality. Whether Crane knew or did not know at first hand about the consecrated nightmare of war is secondary to the fact that he had experienced some event in which massive fears in the presence of imminent danger were produced. The athletic contest comes immediately to mind, since Crane himself draws the comparison: "The psychology is the same. The opposite team is the enemy tribe." His imagery of conflict seems mainly to be drawn from sports. At least one psychologist has commented on sports as an activity in which defense mechanisms are as observable as they are in anxiety-ridden neurotics; but anyone who has ever known the fine agony that precedes an athletic event needs no professional backing to corroborate Crane's perceptions.

Anxiety is classically described as "undischarged excitation," an emotional state attendant on the expectation of some failure, loss, or threat to the body or mind, in which the impulse toward flight is, at least for the moment, checked, or futile. Its referents are varied, environmental or psychic, but the feelings of mental and physical discomfort that anxiety arouses are known and constant. Freud discerns three basic danger situations conducive to anxiety: the fear of the loss of love, the fear of castration, and the loss of social or superego esteem—these anxiety situations being capable of infinite translations in adult life into situations which may plausibly warrant anxiety. Loss of love may range in apostolic succession from mother to nanny to mistress, the fear of castration from father's hardhanded discipline to the oppressor's wrong, and the loss of social or superego esteem from the agons of the chamber pot to "disgrace with fortune and men's eyes."

If anxiety attaches itself to three realms of activity, anxiety has also varied forms of relief, of which several will command our attention. Anxiety has been described as an anticipatory emotion, a mental preparation for danger. Given some motor discharge for the tensions of such a state, anxiety dissipates itself in purposeful activity. Deprived of motor activity, the body, as the psychoanalytic metaphor has it, is "flooded" by unmastered excitation, and the response is panic—mindless flight or paralysis. In the program Ernest Hemingway has set up for the good soldier, it is between the first and the second phases of his experience of war that panic may supervene. In *The Red Badge of Courage*, likewise, it is after Henry Fleming, his anxieties at their spurious ease, has been lulled by a sense of his invulnerability and apparent victory and bodily fatigue, that he is taken by surprise and flees from the battle. He has surrendered to panic.

Cowardice and courage are imprecise public entities; fear (and I use the word as a more dynamic synonym for anxiety) is a strictly personal emotion and may lie, like libido, at the roots of love or hate, behind either cowardice or courage. The central problem becomes, ultimately, the mastering of fear, for which cowardice and courage come to represent mere extremes of adjustment to fear—and a very bad one since it represents the total abdication of the ego from the problem of preserving itself. But there are other, less drastic adjustments which manage to a more or less successful degree to preserve the integrity of the individual, and among these is to be found Henry Fleming's relief from "the red sickness of battle."

The mastering of fear anterior to the mastering of a danger situation involves inevitably the denial, not only of the fear, but of the situation which has produced the fear. The technics of denial, described as counterphobic defenses, are in some respects literally charms against danger, in that one adopts an attitude toward a situation which then will presumably control it. Such an attitude is plainly a regressive one, involving the denial of the world in its most palpable reality when the ego cannot master it. The psychic adaptation to external danger and internal anxiety is a recourse to those mental processes which either ignore reality or finally substitute a system of delusions linked to reality only as magic formulae are linked to the phenomena they control.

A study of Henry Fleming's ordeal reveals, as I have suggested, a medically valid depiction of the psychology of fear. Such a study follows, too, allowing for certain interstitial variations within the catagories the author sets up, Ernest Hemingway's description of a process by which the civilian becomes the good soldier. But *The Red Badge of Courage*, and let us add Hemingway's *A Farewell to Arms*, describe not merely a generic response to danger, but an idiosyncratic and ultimately moral reaction to violence.

Generally speaking, a man becomes a veteran at the expense of a certain emotional and moral finesse. The alternatives of sheer self-preservative panic flight, reckless self-sacrifice, and a sensitivity to the suffering of others are all denied him. The veteran soldier is prudently aggressive, merciless toward his enemies, and loyal to his comrades; he is primitive, a Fortinbras rather than a Hamlet. Neither Crane nor Hemingway appears to have made any such sacrifice of emotional and moral finesse. It is interesting that Hemingway should choose "the boy Sir Philip Sidney" as the ultimate product of the military process. Sidney, it will be remembered, died not in a charge but in an act of compassion: "Poor fellow, thy necessity is greater than mine." Hemingway himself began his career in the army as an ambulance corpsman rather than as a combatant. The novel which most directly incorporates his own war experience shows us a lieutenant, Frederick Henry, a non-combatant ambulance officer, whose revulsion at the meaninglessness of the slaughter he witnesses leads him finally, as another one of Hemingway's characters puts it, to "make a separate peace."

Without doing much more than muse on the identity of surname and Christian name and the reversal of the initials of Henry Fleming and Frederick Henry, I should like to consider Henry Fleming in the light of both an extended study of the psychology of fear and the suggestive headings that Hemingway offers us from *The Torrents of Spring*.

One is aware, in *The Red Badge of Courage*, that an individual, unique characterization threads its way through the studiously generalized experience suggested by the contrivedly anonymous and unbounded framework of the novel. The "youthful private," in spite of the suggestion, finally, that the field is checkered with such types, is perceptibly styled out of the class to which belong the "tall soldier" and the "loud soldier," the "tattered man" and the "cheery man." It is true that the ordeal he undergoes and, to a certain extent his responses, are true to type, but at a significant juncture he exhibits a unique deviation from the standard that the armies propose as their norms. We return, in short, as we do with Hemingway, to the literary hero rather than the military hero.

"First, you were brave," Hemingway writes, "because you didn't think anything could hit you because you yourself were something special, and you knew that you could never die."

In every group of men confronted by a common danger (and this may include athletes as well as soldiers) morale is a massive denial of danger, an assurance of invulnerability, a coral atoll of security built up out of many individual solutions to the problem of personal fear and one's ability to face danger with grace born of a sense of being "something special." Crane's novel begins with a survey of men, a varied lot, constructing mental earthworks of security for themselves. At the beginning of the novel we find Henry Fleming constructing his private fantasy of invulnerability out of his schoolboy experience of life, in which he has learned that war is a matter of the past, a "Greek-like struggle," a "blue demonstration," the academic strategies noted earlier in connection with the spectatorial role. Nothing can happen, Henry Fleming tells himself, because the war is a Homeric archaism, removed from the present. The very fact of the war itself is ingeniously projected into the past and into literature. Such a stratagem bears comparison, does it not, with Tolstoy's use of such a projection in *The Death of Ivan Ilych*, when Ivan Ilych tries to project, unsuccessfully, the fact of his death to the syllogism of Caius's mortality in "Kiezewetter's *Logic*"? As Freud observes, noting the easy expendability of lives in literature and the pleasure we take in these painless fatalities, war challenges "this conventional treatment of death."

A second personal adjustment on Fleming's part involves another projection, this time the projection of his own fears onto his friend Wilson, the "loud soldier." One way of collecting reassurances is to impute fear and cowardice to others. He is frightened; I am not. Wilson and Fleming exhibit both sides of the same counterfeit coin. Fleming impugns Wilson's show of bravery and assurance by attributing his own fears, quite accurately, to Wilson and so intimidating him. Wilson, on the other hand, is denying his fears by acting out, magically, the victory he wants desperately to be reassured of. The one proceeds by disparagement, the other by self-encouragement to the same temporary sense of security. "Gee rod! how we will thump 'em!"

A few hours later, Wilson, confessing himself "a gone coon" less inhibited about expressing his fear, speaks Fleming's anxieties *for* him just as the brigade goes into action.

But these are minor adaptations, which exhaust themselves in discharges of irritability on Fleming's part, in accesses of morbid despair on Wilson's. The momentous process in Fleming's ordeal is removed from these incidentals, although his relationship with Wilson in particular deserves and will receive further mention. Rather, a continuous and unified structure of identifications and relationships carries Fleming through his ordeal and to the threshold of his personal deliverance.

What makes Crane's grasp of the psychology of soldiering something less than miraculous, yet a marvel of intuition, involves his recognition of the subtle affinities between adolescent strivings in the toils of the Oedipal family involvement, and the regressive atmosphere of the military situation. Crane, we must suppose, flung his youth into the retort out of which *The Red Badge of Courage* emerged, making use of, indeed advertising, the relationship between adolescent fantasies of deadly struggle and real violence to create a novel about the experiences of war. In Fleming we see represented a young man attempting to throw off the benevolent swaddlings of his strong-minded, protective mother and the atmosphere of school. He seeks, like Sohrab, to demonstrate his manhood in that ultimate proving ground of manhood, the battle, before a nebulous image of the father whom he barely remembers and who for that reason is everywhere and everyone who breathes authority or assurance. The real drama of the novel lies not so much in the achievement by Henry Fleming of courage (that, as we shall see, is suppositious) as in the extent to which his particular and separate peace with the "red sickness of battle" is rigidly determined by his character.

Army life (and I add, for the last time, any similar group activity) encourages an extension of regressive aims. It provides a moratorium on maturity. The stereotype of the escape from responsibility into the Foreign Legion is well known, and it is more than a schoolboy's dream. Otto Fenichel, for example, describes the "infantilization" that takes place in the mental lives of individual soldiers. The army becomes the institutionalized version of both the protective and the punishing parents. In exchange for giving up his independence the soldier entrusts his life and well-being to his superiors, fashioning the relationship out of its analogy with his earlier dependence. It is a trust, Fenichel observes, "which may give place to a sudden and severe disappointment."

Henry Fleming's sense of invulnerability gives place to such a disappointment at the moment the enemy troops re-form and advance against him. It can be explained in terms of the extension of the Oedipal situation. The unconscious irony of *The Red Badge of Courage* lies in the fact that Henry Fleming never does throw off his swaddling bands. He extends their courage. To consider only the events between the opening of the novel to his running away from the battle, we may observe that he has found his mother again in the collective activity of the army, and has found his father in those men Crane isolates, now here, now there, who represent aggression, assurance, and convey a sense of their omnipotence.

Just as a mother, by holding her fearful child's hand, shares her presumed omnipotence with the child, so Henry Fleming, when the battle forms, is engulfed in the collective security of the regiment. The metaphors of domesticity and enclosure describe his safety. The regiment is a "composite monster"; he was "in a moving box." Images of the schoolroom, the farmyard, the world of women, pile up: the officers are like "scolding" birds and "schoolmistresses," the soldiers are like women trying on "bonnets"—all these represent desperate attempts to master the alien, wholly fearsome situation with the verbal magic of metaphor.

It is more, though, than a matter of metaphor, which leaves the subject still a little vantage point of individuality. Crane draws still another insight from intuition and recognizes that the maternal embrace does not stop at symbols of enclosure; it demands some ultimate complicity on the part of the man. Maternal omnipotence is a passive virtue, an invitation to lie down. The suggestion of sleep and self-forgetfulness, as we shall see later, invites the unwary to confuse death itself with some final form of invulnerability. This invitation becomes finally the crucial experience in *The Red Badge of Courage*, and its resolution for Henry Fleming becomes his inevitable response to it.

The rhythm of the novel may be described as an alternation of sleeps and wakings on the part of Henry Fleming. It may, in these terms, be described as an illustration of the Schopenhauerian conflict between the principle of individuation and the slumbering Will, or between the primordial Female in her passivity and the striving Male principle. Henry Fleming's first "battle sleep" relieves him of the agonizing burden of self-consciousness he had borne in the preceding days. He loses concern with himself "in the common crisis." He is part of the "battle brotherhood," he is a "little finger on a hand."

Psychoanalysis, not always happy in the terminology it uses to describe phenomena, has hit upon a term that does poetic justice to the sensation of collective, ecstatic omnipotence that Crane describes, which are characteristic of the religious, patriotic, and other concerted activities of human beings. It is the "oceanic reunion," a feeling technically referred to as secondary narcissism. It represents an attempt to recapitulate the sense, now outgrown, of omnipotence felt by the infant whose libido has no object but itself (primary narcissism). In secondary narcissism it is the parent or his symbol who renews this sense of power, this sense of an "oceanic" (biology would suggest amniotic) reunion. One holds the Great Mother Herself by the hand. One regresses, psychically, to the community between the mother and the child at her breast, when the infant takes, along with her milk, the omnipotent mother herself into its body. It is the fantasy latent in the dying speech of Shakespeare's Cleopatra, when the serpent at her breast becomes at once the child nursing, who "sucks the nurse asleep," and the nurse who lulls the child. As it synthesizes itself out of the heat and unanimity of battle, Henry Fleming achieves briefly his oceanic reunion.

"Then you found out different," writes Hemingway. "You were really scared then, but if you were a good soldier you functioned the same as before. Then after you were wounded and not killed, with new men coming on and going through your old processes, you hardened and became a good, hard-boiled soldier."

Henry Fleming's panic occurs when he experiences his first surprised disappointment, that in his "battle sleep" his invulnerability is not unassailable. It is material to our understanding of his unconscious denial of fear to note that on all occasions when he fights, he fights like a child in a fantasy of war, firing without aiming, at a "phantom enemy." The prospects of actual conflict with real men like himself, capable of retaliation, jar him awake from his dream of perfect immunity. In his narcissistic world, he is alone, "something special," enclosed in the mother. External objects owe their existence to his will, tractable or else intolerably insurrectionary. The enemy must fall dead on command.

In his waking interim, however, it is no such matter, and in the hours following his flight certain unconscious recognitions and revisions take place in him conditioned by external events, the most important of which is the death of Jim Conklin. It is possible now to consider elements which lie within this "moving box" of maternal omnipotence. These will include certain relations and identifications, as well as a certain sinister latency connected with what I have described as the maternal invitation to "lie down."

In Oedipal terms we may epitomize the situation in this way: maternal omnipotence promises safety without effort on the part of the son. The powerful, authoritarian father, himself omnipotent, apotheosized by Crane in his brilliant expressionistic description of "the gigantic figure of the colonel on a gigantic horse," framed "black and patternlike" (difficult, I suggest, to reconcile with the "black rider" as Berryman sees him) against the sun, introduces a sterner note of duty. The mood is active, strenuous, and dominated by the drives of conscience, and the conscience in this case is the colonel internalized.

What happens to Henry Fleming on the first day of battle amounts to a debacle of family relations. The mother has failed him; the Rebels fought back. He has failed his father, the gigantic colonel. Henry is plunged into a limbo of nullified relationships and ponders desperate remedies, rationalizations which offer slight comfort and do not touch the profound psychic adaptations which must take place. On the one hand, the mother has cast him out into the autonomous world of self-determination; on the other hand, the father, as remote on his horse as one of those patriarchal absolutes Franz Kafka is good at depicting, points an accusing finger at Henry, as coward.

We have so far discussed Henry Fleming in his role as son to the neglect of his relationship with his brothers-in-law, and even his foes, who constitute the siblings in this extension of the family. I have mentioned Wilson and Jim Conklin only briefly, indicating the extent to which Wilson represents the minor variation on Henry Fleming's fears, and Conklin some standard by which he can measure himself. Both men, in fact the whole regiment below the rank of officer, as well as the enemy, may be designated the siblings of Henry Fleming, and, as siblings, subject to the same vicissitudes as he.

Jim Conklin is, and we need not labor the point, the good soldier, and as such becomes for Henry Fleming his sibling ideal, the son he would like to be, the dutiful son in whom the colonel is well pleased. To discriminate between Jim Conklin and all the rest of Fleming's comrades, we might suggest that Fleming exhibits the tendency of the younger brother to transfer to the eldest some of the love and idealization which would otherwise fall to the father. The travesty of assurance his friend Wilson displays arouses only rivalry and contempt in Henry Fleming; Jim Conklin he loves and admires to the extent that Conklin shows some of the assurance which characterizes the omnipotent parent, yet he remains the sibling in that he too must move on command and is subject to an uncertain fate. He is Fleming's Aristotelian hero.

Let us assume that Henry Fleming both consciously and un-consciously elects Jim Conklin as his ego ideal. The conscious election is apparent enough in the respect Henry shows Conklin as an oracle of the coming battle. The unconscious electives are more dispersed, and their influence more pervasive. To Henry Fleming's conscious perceptions, Jim Conklin presents the model for a sensible, realistic, and above all active role in meeting the ominous threat of the battle. The only trouble is that Henry Fleming is unconsciously predisposed against such a role. He must, as I have suggested before, work his salvation out his own way.

What interests Henry Fleming more than *how* he will do (here Conklin provides a certain template for Henry) is *what* will happen to him. Here Jim Conklin can only direct Henry to an attitude which he can take only on speculation; by living or dying himself he will confirm or deny the fears that beset him. Of the two major anxieties, the loss of life and the loss of esteem, Henry Fleming has repressed the more pressing of the two. It haunts him from the cellarage. I have mentioned, as a sinister latency in the idea of maternal omnipotence, the confusion of death with invulnerability. Fleming's tentative identification with Jim Conklin is complicated by the unconscious appeal this confusion makes to him. Before the battle he thinks: "Regarding death thus out of the corner of his eye, he conceived it to be nothing but rest and he was filled with the momentary astonishment that he should have made an extraordinary commotion about the mere matter of getting killed." The idea, not only of rest, but of invulnerability, manifests itself to him when he sees the dead soldier: "The invulnerable dead man forced a way for himself." The troops must march around his inviolable body.

Now, although there seems to be some continuity between Fleming's bland attitude toward death before the battle and his reckless wish to die after his return, certain recognitions have intervened, bound up with the fate of Jim Conklin and his own shameful flight. "He jests at scars who never felt a wound" is the spirit which governs Fleming's first *conscious* reaction to the thought of his own death. He is too thoroughly entrenched in his own sense of invulnerability to be able to accept the idea of personal destruction as anything beyond a verbal concept. There is nothing to prevent his standing up, like Jim Conklin, to the enemy.

It is when the enemy rises up against him that the idea of death, and with it the consequences of being Jim Conklin, occur to him. The true, rather than the mythical, implications of the descent into the grave appear, unrelieved by the compassionate veil that regression throws over the experience of death. Here, suddenly, there is no "moving box," no collective security; there is only one's own cold-blooded mutilation. We confront here the permanent paradox of men at war who are most manly when they have become demonic children fighting under the aegis of some protective deity. In Homer's *Iliad*, Achilles defeats Hector when the former becomes the infantile berserker. Deprived of the concerns of adult life, he is more capable of the ultimate effort of war. Hector fights like a man against him, incapable of the ecstatic sense of immunity Achilles derives from the identification grief induces with Patroclus and its discharge as rage. Hector's recognition of the regressive adaptations of battle makes him refuse to return to his wife the night before he is killed. Such, too, was the impulse of Uriah the Hittite, when he fought against the Ammonites. Admittedly, Henry Fleming is no Hector, but, as I have suggested earlier, his youth and his predisposed temperament render him unfit for the aggressions war demands. The seasoned soldier, we are told, converts his fears of death into hatred and aggression. He will suffer death in order to inflict it. Toward the dead there exists not a sense of compassion, but a sense of scorn (repressed naturally) that they have succumbed, and a wish for revenge, whose magic objective, like Achilles' sacrifice of twelve Trojans to the shade of Patroclus, is to restore one's fallen comrades to some nebulous form of life.

The Henry Fleming who shrieks and runs from the corpse in the "religious half light" of the woods is not the Henry Fleming who earlier had made his way around the "invulnerable dead man." Nor is he the young man who a moment before has found nature to be a "woman with a deep aversion to tragedy." His fear of death has been completely activated by his flight and is for the moment denied the palliation it requires.

The death of Jim Conklin, including the peculiar ceremony that accompanies it, is the turning point, but only the turning point, in Fleming's slow coming-about to his final mastery of fear. He turns again after Conklin's death to the old task of mastering his fear, but this time his technics are limited by his experience and by the unconscious latencies in his identification with Jim Conklin. We may summarize (without, however, shirking an explanation) Fleming's reaction to Jim Conklin's death by saying that Henry overcomes his fear of death by the strength of identification with Conklin. Once again death has been domesticated; Jim Conklin becomes retroactively all dead men. The living in this ocean of the dead and dying are anomalous to the normal order of things, and the old invitation to sleep takes on more somber tones. In his death, seeking with antique formality (*Oedipus at Colonnus* comes immediately to mind) his fated piece of earth, Jim Conklin directs Fleming to an intuition that was inchoate when he saw the "invulnerable corpse" and conceived of death as "nothing but rest."

Fleming's actions immediately following Conklin's death are symptomatic of unconscious adjustment. His first thoughts involving his disgrace, are along the lines of what has come to be called the "world destruction fantasy." It accompanies, paradoxically enough, that cozy sense of collective security that men experience in the face of a common crisis. The fantasy amounts to a projection outward of the fear of personal destruction, the establishment of an inverted norm, like the felicities of the early dynastic Egyptian underworld where the deceased exclaims, "I am the boy in the fields, the young man of the city is my name." Fleming briefly considers such a world destruction: "In a defeat there would be a roundabout vindication of himself. A defeat of the army had suggested itself to him as a means of escape from the consequences of his fall."

He again seeks for the reunion with omnipotence he had briefly enjoyed, but now it is complicated by his recognition that it cannot be his without a struggle. We may describe it again in terms of childhood experience, terms sanctioned by Fleming's own predisposition to revert to certain patterns of childhood dependence. Maternal omnipotence is passive. It lulls the sense of individuation. Like Jocasta it mocks the reproaches of oracles and denies the existence of duties and dangers. It thrives in a fatherless world. But the way to this reunion with the mother is blocked (and the organization and function of an army at war are a magnification of this process) by a stern and equally omnipotent father, with whom reunion is possible only through a process of imitation and identification and, if this process proves impossible, through an act of self-immolation. In Oedipal terms, this is a reunion through a masochistic identification with the mother.

We recall that Henry Fleming's mother has invoked his dead father's memory along with her own prayers that he will behave honorably. He has, because of his youth, and his tendency to accept the role of the dependent son, fled from the battle. His dead father cries from his conscience; the gigantic colonel glares from his horse;

Jim Conklin reproaches him from his burial place; his mother mutely waits with folded hands for him to act, since it is to her, in any case, he must return. The question his dilemma raises is *How?* His cowardice has driven him from the charmed circle his comrades inhabit and from any substantial identification with the colonel.

The hazard of an identification with some omnipotent being, or some ego idea, lies in, as we have seen, the fact that such figures tend to become confused with fate itself, a fate in which one has trusted. The loss of such a being (e.g., the initial scattering of the regiment) is in itself traumatic. Such powerful figures, when they are sufficiently individualized, (the maternal army is too vast, too oceanic, the colonel too awesome, too remote, to become more than titanic abstractions— "the Indefinite Cause, whatever it was responsible for him") are describable as "magic helpers" who take over the executive funtions of the individual soldier who needs then only blindly to obey in order to be preserved.

The ordering of events between the time of Conklin's death and Fleming's rejoining the regiment impinges directly on the loss of Conklin as "magic helper." Fleming's irritable rejection of the pitifully wounded "tattered man" is as symptomatic as it is responsible. Henry's grief at the loss of Jim Conklin is exacerbated by the fact that Fleming has lost his most accessible source of omnipotence. He cannot help; he must be helped. The second event that takes place is understandable in the regressive logic of neurosis. Without ceasing to wish for and finally to obtain a new magic helper, Fleming identifies himself with Jim Conklin. But it is a qualified identification. He tries for a moment to see himself "throw off himself and become a better . . . a blue, desperate figure leading lurid charges with one knee forward and a broken blade high—a blue, determined figure standing before a crimson and steel assault, getting calmly killed on a high place before the eyes of all. He thought of the magnificent pathos of his own body." The vision fails him: "He had no rifle; he could not fight with his hands, said he resentfully to his plan." Again the fine ironic play between the "pretentious and the scared."

What is wrong with this fantasied identification with Jim Conklin is the element of aggression involved. I have indicated certain consistencies in Henry Fleming's character. They begin now to take positive shape. The one major consistency is his constant deflection away from aggression toward the masochistic submission to fate and authority. It is out of this most unpromising nettle that Henry Fleming must pluck the flower safely. His identification with Jim Conklin turns not on Jim Conklin's presumably heroic fight but upon his being dead. What obsesses Fleming for a while is the idea of his death in the presence of some Awful Superior. Crane very subtly indicates the ambivalence and temporary quality of this obsession by a telling use of the limited point of view. "He now *thought that he wished* he was dead. He believed that he envied those men whose bodies lay strewn over the grass of the fields" (my italics).

In his identification with Jim Conklin, Fleming has discovered momentarily a way out of his disgrace and separation, a method of placating his conscience. One has only to die before the father, the colonel on the horse.

> It was clear to him that his final and absolute revenge was to be achieved by his dead body lying, torn and glittering, upon the field. This was to be a poignant retaliation upon the officer who had said "mule drivers" and later "mud diggers," for in all the wild graspings of mind for a unit responsible for his sufferings and commotions he always seized upon the man who had dubbed him wrongly. And it was his idea, vaguely formulated, that his corpse would be for those eyes a great and salt reproach.

This consummate act of moral masochism, this offering of oneself, as Freud puts it, as a "willing victim to fate," is under certain circumstances the neurotic solution to Oedipal strivings. If the process by which one comes finally to identify one's interests with the father and so effect some atonement with him is interrupted, aggressions developed on the way to such an atonement direct themselves against their possessor. The alternative becomes a flight in the direction of a passive, feminine submission to the "good" father image, to a point where the filial is equivalent to the maternal position, as regards the father.

We may regard this new anxiety (over the loss of paternal esteem) and the defense against it as representing a higher stage of development from Henry Fleming's initial fear of having lost maternal protection, a mere concern for safety. Now conscience, the superego, has come onto the scene, and Fleming is posed between the imperatives of his impulse to fly and his sense of guilt, which demands expiation in the form of his death.

The connection between Fleming's original sense of immunity to danger and his present dangerous resolution to die forthwith rests in his need to be reunited with the potent superior beings, both maternal and paternal, who have either abandoned him or cast him out. Personal safety has gone by the board; with Jim Conklin as the precursor, Fleming may now pursue honor in the cannon's mouth. Thus his present urge to destroy himself is the reverse side of the immunity obtained through identification with a superior. The lost omnipotence is renewed in the very act of being destroyed or in destroying oneself. This is particularly true in situations where one's self-esteem has suffered a severe blow by virtue of some act of cowardice which has separated one from the group.

"The attempt to get rid of the pressure from the superego," writes Otto Fenichel, "is the aim of all self-destruction. . . . The ascetic pride of self-destruction and self-sacrifice is for the purpose of regaining participation in the omnipotence of the powerful authority figure, or its representative in the superego. It is a passive-receptive merging with the omnipotent person."

The wish to be destroyed for the sake of forgiveness and reconciliation is augmented by a consideration which overdetermines the desire for death—the identification with Jim Conklin that can meaningfully be interpreted as an act of mourning, the expression of a wish to be reunited with the dead. To this intense wish to participate in the life and death of Jim Conklin belongs the only wound Henry Fleming is to suffer. It would be ridiculous to explain the minor head wound he receives as absolutely of his own devising, but the use he makes of it allows no ambiguity as to its function. After he has been struck, "he went tall soldier fashion." He imagined secluded spots where he could fall and be "unmolested." He is, in fact, Jim Conklin.

Part of the grim comedy of Henry Fleming's patent defenses against fear and disgrace lies in the fact that they pass off in repetitious fantasies which must be practically unsuccessful in warding off these anxieties. He survives his own daydream of a heroic death. His wound, to which he has been masochistically receptive, is after all a safe, mitigated version of Jim Conklin's mortal wounding, a spanking rather than a death.

What Henry Fleming returns to finally is Henry Fleming, in need of the magic helper he has lost. He regresses always, in terms of erogenous zones, to the toothless stage of oral receptivity. It is a stage which finds its characterological foundation in the early sucking stage of infancy. Here, aggressiveness is replaced by an infinite willingness to receive. Self-assertion and independence are replaced by self-abasement and dependence, or by an intuition of luck and immunity from the dangers that others must face alone. Such helplessness is a component of mourning, institutionally recognized in the apparent incongruity of the funeral feast prepared for the mourners. Henry Fleming's thoughts return, after Conklin's death, after Henry has been struck, to the magic helper he left behind him—his mother, and particularly to "certain meals his mother had cooked at home, in which those dishes of which he was particularly fond had occupied prominent positions." He remembers, too, swimming with his school friends in the river. More than hunger and thirst induce these memories; they are the yearnings of loss and separation from breast and womb. Just as the mother returns to nostalgic reflection, the "cheery man" comes along in actuality to return Fleming to his regiment. He is recognizedly the answer to an unconscious need. He "seemed to possess a wand of a magic kind." One is led to suspect, by the ease with which this stranger finds his way back to Fleming's regiment, that the extent to which Fleming is lost is relative to his own regressive loss of orientation. He has become in this bleak interim the little boy entire.

"Then came the second crack," writes Hemingway, "which is much worse than the first, and then you began doing good deeds and being the boy Sir Philip Sidney and storing up treasures in heaven. At the same time of course functioning always the same as before. As if it were a football game."

Looking back over the events that have taken place thus far, we are aware that a certain dramatic unity has asserted itself, governed by the intricate consistencies of Henry Fleming's character and driving inferentially toward some inevitable conclusion. With mythical simplicity the fact of death and the need to face it present themselves to our frightened neophyte until, all denials and rationalizations failing him, he turns and flees towards it, whereupon it loses its terror for him and he returns to life.

With Henry Fleming we are in the epic tradition of the *Gilgamesh* and the *Odyssey*, whose heroes descend into Hell to rescue Enkidu or learn their fates, and learn among other things that death is neither blissful nor noble, and return more resolutely to life. Within other contexts, but I think in ways that psychologically have striking affinities, D. H. Lawrence has described the "drift towards death" and the recoil from it in *Sons and Lovers* and *Women in Love*, and Thomas Mann has dealt at great length with such an experience in Hans Castorp's long dalliance beside the "ocean of time" and his final emergence.

The strictly psychoanalytic view of these events has revealed an equally impressive unity, even more rigidly determined by the character of the hero than by the timeless and intrinsically mythical quality of armed conflict. Henry Fleming transfers his Oedipal strivings to his need to remain within the charmed circle of maternal protection, his inability to meet the stern demands of the paternal superego, his self-destructive bid for reconciliation and forgiveness, and his need for magic helpers, to the field of battle.

It may be thought that now in this developmental schedule Henry Fleming should emerge the happy warrior. But about the hero of *The Red Badge of Courage* as about the hero of *Oedipus Rex* it is enough to say that he emerges without claiming the superhumanity of perfect adjustment. We can say about both heroes that they discover the conduct proper to their native qualities as men. There are, in fact, certain affinities between Henry Fleming and Oedipus that I shall touch upon.

I have described the rhythm of *The Red Badge of Courage* as a rhythm of sleeping and waking, "battle sleep" preceded and followed by a period of self-conscious anxiety. It is equally describable as a rhythm of reunions and alienations in connection with some omnipotent superior power. It may finally and most comprehensively be described as a rhythm of alternating "flights."

Hamlet, too thoughtful to be a hero, considers

> Whether 'tis nobler in the mind to suffer
> The slings and arrows of outrageous fortune
> Or to take arms against a sea of troubles
> And by opposing end them.

If we recognize the *Hamlet* of Freud's and Ernest Jones's studies as well as Shakespeare's play, and grant that his anxieties are in excess of the realistic motives of revenge for murder and usurpation, then we realize that what Hamlet is considering here is not a plan of attack against a real adversary, but a defense against his own nebulous anxieties; not how to change his fate, but how to face his fears. He exhibits throughout the play his neurotic ability to face real problems realistically, and his behavior consists of alternate "flights" to activity and passivity which are productive of nothing but useless murders and unhappiness and a morbid paralysis of will.

Anxiety has been described as a state of preparedness for a danger situation; panic and terror as disorganized responses to unexpected dangers, the "flooding" of the system with undischarged anxiety. Both states are liable to exaggeration into attitudes of hair-trigger readiness and the most abject helplessness, the one to prevent the other. Hamlet's electric gibes and plans and his inability to premediate a definite coup are symptomatic of his state. Helplessness under certain circumstances, the loss of volitional powers, or the illusion of such a loss, becomes the most painful of feelings. It is, we intuitively surmise, because the survival of the ego depends upon our feeling at all times that we take an active part in the ordering of our destinies. Those ecstatic moments of collective self-determination, which come in our oceanic reunion with others, are of necessity temporary states.

In a mind overcharged with anxiety, denied the pathological release of mania or unconsciousness, one is driven to deny either the anxiety or the situation which gave rise to the anxiety. The flight to activity denies fear and danger by the paradoxical strategy of exposing one to the very thing one fears. To prevent and forestall the terror of surprise and the annihilative sense of being a hapless victim, one seeks actively the feared situation, preferring even destruction to the dread of destruction. Thus Ovid is being psychologically accurate in his description of fear-crazed men in a plague-ridden city who

> Hung themselves
> Driving the fear of death away by death,
> By going out to meet it.

Such exposures and responses to danger are not always so drastic.

If one survives the initial onslaught of outrageous fortune, one then returns to meet it again compulsively, to prove to oneself that the thing one feared might happen did not in actuality happen, while all the while the original and unresolved anxiety forbids final proof. In effect one strives to realize, to enclose within a rigid framework of intention, what had originally been a unique and unforeseen accident. Thus one may be induced to rush blindly into a battle because of a profound fear of battle, or to incur in some mitigated form what might first have been a serious injury.

I have discussed, in connection with the "magic helper," the regression of Henry Fleming at that point to the stage of oral receptivity, a passive suckling stage. The flight to activity similarly elects an oral regressive stage in which mastery is achieved not by suckling helplessness, but by a destructive biting. Such destructive biting, as it applies here, finds a felicitous apposition in the Icelandic sagas that often depict the "berserker," the bloodlusting fighter (who is very often defeated by his more prudent antagonist), literally champing on the edge of his own shield in his murderous frenzy.

Here the flight to activity involves the primitive logic of becoming the thing or the person one fears and then proceeding to intimidate others. Reassurance is bound up with the obsessive display of fierceness; seeming *is* being, pretensions are genuine. The encouragement of one's friends is merely a benevolent variation on identification with the aggressor. One offers one's friends the encouragement one stands desperately in need of for one's self. Such cheers and threats are as readily observable on the playing fields of Eton as they are on the battlefield of Waterloo. In all these instances of the flight to activity the stress is laid upon the active as synonymous with the intentionality of the act performed. Perhaps the best instance of volition *in extremis* is afforded by the ancient world's recognition that suicide was the most dignified form of execution in capital crimes.

In connection with the flight to activity an oblique reference to the collection of trophies (the cups, banners, scalps of sports and battles) will bear interesting fruit when we apply it to Henry Fleming's final appearance under the hard-won banners he has collected. Otto Fenichel remarks that the trophy is a palpable attestation to the fact that one has in reality "run a risk without incurring the consequences."

Having outlined the flight to passivity in terms of Henry Fleming's readiness to accept protection, to yield rather than to advance, we may now chart in their alternating order the flights he undertakes and describe his final synthesis. "Regarding death thus out of the corner of his eye," by what valid means does Henry Fleming master his fears? Whatever toy slings and rubber-tipped arrows of a not-so-outrageous fortune he has suffered in the past, he has developed a characteristic response to them, which persists in his experience of war, and which finally perfects itself to become the ark of his salvation.

The true direction of Henry Fleming's flight is, we may safely say, towards passivity. The exigencies of his situation drive him into activity, but it is inevitably a spurious flight, a pantomime of activity from which he turns back with a sense of relief, back to his old dependencies. To say, however, that there is no final and elevated stasis awarded him in the role is to ignore both the course of the novel and the psychological directive that underlies it. The *mathema*, the education of King Oedipus, is an education not only in submission to the gods, but in his own identity. The "self-made," active man of scene 1 takes refuge in his "unthinkable fate" at the last because at the last he knows who he is, and therefore what his fate is. Fleming, at the end of his ordeal, accepts his role as the passive spectator of the conflict because it is entirely in accordance with his sense of himself.

To stretch the mantle of King Oedipus a little further over *The Red Badge of Courage*, I would suggest still another analogy. Oedipus's arrogance early in the play derives from the protection and encouragement he receives from his wife-mother. Jocasta offers him a false security. His prophetic anxieties, his father's blood crying from the oracles, and his own conscience lead him to self-discovery, expiation, and a final abdication of any active control of fate. His accounts are rendered in full.

Henry Fleming's activity first proceeds from his being in the maternal security of the regiment. He is the spoiled only child of an indulgent and protective mother. His trial flights to activity are tentative and mean-spirited. He intimidates poor Wilson for his own aggrandizement, just as Wilson drowns his fears under his own loud self-encouragement. Jim Conklin holds out an image of some integrity, but the battle destroys it as a possibility, for Fleming's conduct on the first day of battle is the aimless destructiveness of oral sadism. The mere appearance on the horizon of his consciousness of hostile siblings renders him again impotent, passive. He is suddenly wearing "invisible mittens" (the image will be used in other stories); death is "about to thrust him between the shoulder blades"; "destruction threatened him from all points"; and he takes to ignominious flight.

If he is not Henry Fleming the gallant soldier, who is he? His fear of destruction has alienated him from the false security of the mother; his cowardice awakens the sense of the paternal reproach. The father dominates any attempts, first of all, to excuse his cowardice to himself—"he had fled early because of his superior powers of perception"—to give his flight a virile framework of intention, and second, to expiate his guilt by taking belatedly Jim Conklin's road to dusty death. Both these alternate flights to activity are abandoned, as in a moment of physical and moral exhaustion Fleming yields himself up passively to the magic helper, the "cheery man," who leads him back to his regiment, the helpless, dependent, lost boy.

The subsequent stages of Fleming's development introduce two new elements, one of them undreamed of in *Oedipus Rex*. This final act of *The Red Badge of Courage* may be said now to become a *fraternal* competition for the love, protection, and esteem of *both* parents, in which Fleming's role is qualified by its being exclusively filial and submissive. His flight to passivity acquires an ethical dimension. This does not at first seem apparent until we measure his new-found valor against his new-found protectress, the flag, in terms of his inner satisfactions.

Fleming's second stand in battle is suspiciously like the first; the differentia is the degree of anger he feels, and this can be accounted for in terms of revenge. Again there is the mindless destructivity, the uncontrollable shooting at "tormentors" who are more like vermin than men. He continues to fire long after the enemy has retreated. Again there is, at the end, the sense of impotence— "in a dream it occurred to the youth that his rifle was an impotent stick" —a sense that previously had sent him into flight.

Gregory Zilboorg, writing about troop morale in World War II, describes the sanction of anger in the process:

> It is a well observed fact that "green" troops become "seasoned" as soon as they become angry—that is, as soon as they begin to convert their fear of death into hatred and aggression. This usually happens after the baptism of fire, not so much because the soldiers become accustomed to the fire of the enemy, but primarily because their anger begins to be aroused after they have lost some of their brothers in combat. It is the mechanism of revenge, of overcoming death by means of murder, that proves to be the most potent psychological force.

It is here, precisely at what would seem to be the moment of his apotheosis as the soldier-hero, that Henry Fleming makes his final adaptation, not to his fears but to his nature, for reasons I assume must ultimately rest with Stephen Crane. Far from being the hardened veteran, Fleming has turned entirely toward the higher moral and softer emotional sensibilities of the noncombatant.

I have described him as being endowed with the "faculties of interest and curiosity" to an extraordinary degree, and with the susceptibilities of youth and sensitivity given to submission to and identification with figures of authority. These qualities are alien to, or rather can only contribute to, "the delirium that encounters despair and death and is heedless and blind to the odds," and may possibly terminate in the same sense of impotence and terror as before.

Those who elect passivity as their release from anxiety are characterized as more dependent upon the power and good will of others. Their aggressions demand their weight in feelings of guilt, and one pays for one's supply of love and security by accepting along with the gratification a certain amount of punishment. As a fighter Fleming knows only delirium. It is only when he sees the flag which he endows obviously with the intermingled trappings of maternity and divinity—"a creation of beauty and invulnerability . . . a goddess . . . a woman, red and white . . . because no harm could come to it he endowed it with power"—that he falls finally and easily into his role. His real pleasure and mastery come when he seizes the flag and is "deeply absorbed as a spectator" of what has now become for him as it was in the beginning, a remote "blue demonstration," with other regiments fighting "as if at a matched game." To the lieutenant rallying the troops, Henry becomes the passive helpmate and builds not an identification but a filial, almost daughterly relationship with the man of action. "Between him and the lieutenant, scolding and near to losing his mind with rage, there was felt a subtle fellowship and equality. They supported each other in all manner of hoarse, howling protests."

As a fighter Fleming's behavior is autistic, infantile. His fraternal competition for the flag is an entirely different matter. It bespeaks relationship, the rivalry of brothers for the love of the parents. The fact that he wrests two flags from the hands of dying color guards and struggles with his friend Wilson for one, subsequently exposing himself to enemy fire, would lead me to postulate a fantasy psychologically equivalent to the facts (the incident is itself the elaboration of a true one): a fantasy in which the younger brother supersedes the elder because of the elder's death or wished-for death, and who then expiates the guilty aggression by taking up the same dangerous position, yet in a passive role. Such a fantasy would then extend the identification I proposed in connection with Jim Conklin, whom Fleming replaces with the clear intention of dying as a "salt reproach" to the colonel. The rival flag is Fleming's trophy to show that he has come through, that he has achieved a new invulnerability, a renewed reunion with the parents.

Read with the concepts stated here in mind, the end of *The Red Badge of Courage* makes somewhat more sense in its repudiation of all that Fleming has struggled to achieve. The close turns away as Fleming turns away from the "red sickness of battle. He had been an animal blistered and sweating in the heat and pain of war." The ending turns away in short from more than cowardice; it turns from "delirium," the "battle sleep," and presumably the bloodshed, to "images of tranquil skies, fresh meadows, cool brooks—an existence of soft and eternal peace." The novel ends not with the formulation of military courage following cowardice, but more with the formulation suggested by Freud in his "Thoughts on War and Death"—that death realized becomes "life-conditioning."

Fleming has succeeded in effecting a sublimation of impulses that had hitherto been blocked or exercised with disastrous effects. He has sacrificed activity without the loss of self-esteem or social alienation. He has fulfilled some socially acceptable ideal conception of himself. What had been an apron has become an aegis; what had been a flight has become an individual choice of mode.

Order in *The Red Badge of Courage*

Norman Lavers

The friendliest critics admit that *The Red Badge of Courage* is patternless—a mere series of brilliant and inconsequent episodes, at best ordered by alternating moods, or rhythmic shifts in direction. Not only that, but there is the problem of intention; did Crane ever make up his mind that his hero, Henry Fleming, *was* a hero? For instance, what have we at the end—sentimentality? Or is that "golden ray of sun" an undercutting of mordant irony?

Crane may not have been able to answer this. I suspect that what we have taken to be problems of structure and intention result partly from neither Henry nor Crane being entirely aware of what he is about. Nonetheless, the story has a firmly articulated structure, and it pursues a consistent course to an unequivocal conclusion. To see this, we have to give Crane's famous imagery our shrewdest attention.

The imagery per se, operating so perfectly on the descriptive level, is not going to concern us here, since this imagery is not unique to Crane; rather, we shall examine—from complementary perspectives— the system underlying, at the point where imagery becomes complexly related to theme, to the attitudes of the characters, and perhaps (though this is less important to our purposes) to Crane's vision of reality.

I shall begin to project this system into relief by exploring Crane's third novel, *George's Mother*, a work which, with *The Red Badge* and "The Open Boat," makes up what I consider the major body of Crane's

From *The University Review* 32, no. 4 (June 1966). © 1966 by the Curators of the University of Missouri.

literary production. Significantly, these three superficially dissimilar works are strikingly parallel in theme and structure.

Crane's brilliant and strangely neglected novel, *George's Mother* had an original title, "A Woman without Weapons"—which provides a clue to Crane's intentions. Evidently he was writing about a woman who wanted to conquer all evil, who wanted to banish sin from the entire universe, and who nevertheless finally cannot even protect her son from the dragon drink. This explains the mock-heroic style with which Crane portrays her. We see this frail woman depicted almost as a female knight in shining armor, gallantly addressing herself to a stove that "lurked in the gloom, red-eyed, like a dragon." The mock-heroic metaphor is extended when we see the mother has transformed her son into one of those fair maids which knights are traditionally set up to defend against calumny, enchantments, and monsters. "Her mind created many wondrous influences that were swooping like green dragons at him."

The reversal of sex roles is only one feature in an overwhelming richness of details inviting the reader to discuss the story in psychoanalytical terms, for Crane, without a single false step, leads us through the history of a "terrible mother" possessing her son all but physically, so that the covert carnal temptations of their relationship have obsessed them both with guilt, paralyzed the son's development, and bred in him what may be reasonably called a latent homosexuality.

This sounds glib, but indeed, had the story been written recently we should probably have accused the writer of having read his Freud too sedulously and prepared too neat a clinical study. Yet the work was written some half-dozen years before Freud's first mention of the Oedipus complex. The story's very neatness makes us believe we are in contact with a Stephen Crane who has his defenses down; thus perhaps we are near the source of his creation, the logical place to begin studying his work.

Let us take provisionally the suggestion that unrecognized incest desires dominate mother and son and see where this suggestion leads us. "There came often a love-light into [his mother's] eyes. The wrinkled, yellow face frequently warmed into a smile of the kind that a maiden bestows upon him who to her is first and perhaps last." George "grew to plan for these glances." By a common device of the unconscious, they have projected their temptations onto external objects—in this case, the chapel where the mother goes to prayer meeting, and the tavern where George drinks. These two places, so different in their outward uses, are in the story symbolically sexual in an identical way. Early in the account George's mother "imagined a woman, wicked and fair, who had fascinated him and was turning his life into a bitter thing. Her mind created many wondrous influences that were swooping like green dragons at him." George, who had heard "the beckoning sirens of drink," thought that "drink and its surroundings were the eyes of a superb green dragon."

The repetition of the "green dragon" would indicate that both looked upon drink as the rival woman. This becomes grotesquely patent when the tavern engulfs him "with a gleeful motion of its two widely smiling lips."

If I seem to be forcing things here, I can make a better case with the chapel. George's mother hugs and wheedles and caresses him in the most coquettish fashion, trying to induce him into her chapel. He puts her off with all the fears and embarrassments of an inexperienced lover, but finally gives in. There is already a public suggestion in that the chapel is described as sitting "humbly between two towering apartment-houses," and, to perfect the picture, we are told that a red street lamp standing in front of the chapel "threw a marvelous reflection upon the wet pavement. It was like the death-stain of a spirit."

Or a blood stain? The noises of the city at this place "suggested an approaching barbaric invasion. The little church, pierced, would die with a fine illimitable scorn for its slayers." George, knees shaking, dreaded the "terrible moment when the doors should swing back," but a small man standing, with anatomical accuracy in the "vestibule . . . pushed the doors aside, and he followed his mother up the center aisle of the little chapel." His immediate sensations are shame and guilt.

The conflict in the story is between George's mother trying to induce him into her chapel, and George's friends trying to induce him into the tavern. The mother understands that drink is her rival: she belongs to the W.C.T.U. But outside her window, standing potently over the scene, is the towering brewery. "Thick smoke came from funnels and spread near it like vast and powerful wings. The structure seemed a great bird, flying . . . a machine of mighty strength." The bird, legendary symbol of masculine spirit, is flying—the symbol in dreams of the sexual act. Is this brewery for George perhaps a symbol of liberation? Will it carry him away from the enchantment his mother holds him in?

With fits and starts, it finally does, and the mother dies. But it is only a qualified freedom, for drink brings him not normal love, but homosexual relationships with a group of men. Ordinary sorts of homosexual undertones are present in their, as in all exclusively male, drinking bouts—but these come to head, I think, at Bleeker's party, where first Jones "made a furious attempt to dance" with him, and a moment later, George reeled with drunkenness, and "Jones grappled him close. He was amazed to find that Jones possessed the strength of twenty horses [those erotic horses which arise so frequently from Crane's unconscious]. He was forced skillfully to the floor." Twice he tries to rise, but he is forced back to the floor again. "It was unspeakable barbarism," perhaps reminiscent of the "barbaric invasion" of the chapel.

George's Mother, concluding with a drunken George guiltily witnessing his mother's death, is the only one of Crane's three major works which seems to end in failure, but I suspect that we have this feeling because the ending is truncated. It is as if *The Red Badge of Courage* were to end with Henry guiltily watching the death of the spectral Jim Conklin. George, too, witnesses the death immediately after fleeing from a battle. All three of Crane's major works follow, more or less completely, more or less explicitly, and with more or less conscious intention on Crane's part, the same pattern. Stated most simply, the pattern is that of separation from the mother in order to achieve full development as an individual.

As is always the case when a really fundamental rhythm is tapped, a number of other patterns, sociological, biographical, mythological, can be superimposed upon it, fitting with great precision. This is only a sign that these patterns all derive from the original. If R. W. Stallman's attempts to fit the Christian myth over this basic pattern seem unsuccessful, it is only because of his consistently misplaced emphasis. Actually, no doubt due to Crane's early religious environment, the movement of his work readily translates into Christian terminology. The pattern leads from (1) a sense of sin, through (2) awareness of mortality, (3) the sacrifice of an innocent, (4) atonement through suffering and "good works" (in a vividly depicted purgatory), to (5) ultimate redemption through self-knowledge.

George's Mother took the first elements of this, George's sin, his contemplation of death (when "dead" drunk), and the sacrifice of his at least outwardly innocent mother. A sequel to the story might have seen his eventual redemption through action as a coming to terms with himself.

In "The Open Boat" we witness the last half of the five-point program: the suffering and good works (in a purgatory—managed by seagull friends—fiendishly designed to allow the sufferers to contemplate the undamned walking about on the unattainable shore) and final redemption. The separation from the mother is represented archetypically in the men's attempts to escape "the fierce old mother" of Whitman, the maternal sea. Without pressing for a homosexual interpretation, I can point out that once more the first step away from the mother is taken with the assistance of other men, with whom the protagonist has an especially close fellow-feeling.

In our earlier glimpse of the correspondent, he "watched the waves and wondered why he was there." He is indignant with the world. He is without sin—why should he be made to suffer? But later, alone with his thoughts at night, his companions sleeping, he is faced not with an imaginary dragon, but with a very real shark which insists on remaining with him "ahead or astern, on one side or the other," literally surrounding his musings.

It is a huge, powerful, beautiful thing to contemplate—but yet dreadful. "He wished one of his companions to awake by chance and keep him company with it." Actually, the captain had been awake and had seen it, and later the cook sees a shark of his own. Only the innocent oiler—he who will be sacrificed—misses seeing a shark. By the time the critical moment is reached when they must try to swim to shore through the heavy surf, the correspondent, now believing in his mortality, feels less innocent, thinking "it is, perhaps, plausible that a man in this situation, impressed with the unconcern of the universe, should see the innumerable flaws of his life, and have them taste wickedly in his mind, and wish for another chance. A distinction between right and wrong seems absurdly clear to him." Awareness of sin, contemplation of death, atonement (through suffering and acts), the sacrifice of the oiler—all these lead to the conclusion in which "the wind brought the sound of the great sea's voice to the men on the shore, and they felt that they could then be interpreters." I have suggested that in at least some of Crane's imagery there is a projectional, or even delusional quality. His typical irony is to have his characters visualize their meager lives in heroic terms, to see the impersonal universe in romantic or hostile dress. Consider for example this poem:

> To the maiden
> The sea was blue meadow,
> Alive with little froth-people
> Singing.

> To the sailor, wreched,
> The sea was dead grey walls
> Superlative in vacancy,
> Upon which nevertheless at fateful time
> Was written
> The grim hatred of nature.

It would seem that the personifications are to be attributed to the moods of the characters. This ironical use of pathetic fallacy is the governing stylistic principle of all Crane's work, and permeates especially the texture of *The Red Badge of Courage,* where it sets the tone for the whole novel.

But it is even more important structurally. By having the imagery reflect the world, not as it is, but as his characters conceive it to be, Crane gives us constant access to the inner states of these characters, and perhaps his style is as much expressionistic as it is impressionistic. From this standpoint one can readily trace a pattern, particularly in the animal imagery of *The Red Badge of Courage,* which shifts with the shifting moods of the protagonist.

If we can identify the imagery as belonging to Henry Fleming, we see that initially he conceives of the two armies as monsters of equal power, equally horrible, perhaps, but with a fascinating beauty. If "the red, eyelike gleam of hostile camp-fires" seemed to him "to be growing larger, as the orbs of a row of dragons, advancing," he saw in his own army "shadows that moved like monsters." His regiment set out "like one of those moving monsters wending with many feet," and "there was an occasional flash and glimmer of steel from the back of all these huge crawling reptiles."

Henry, desperately hoping he will be able to maintain his identity with his dragon, anxiously looks forward to the collision between the hostile monsters, knowing it will show, in one way or another, the degree of his integration. His great concern is that through fear he will lose his identity with this secure monster. He "studied the faces of his companions, ever on the watch to detect kindred emotions. He suffered disappointment." Another monster, hideously disarticulated, was threatening him, a "thousand-tongued fear that would babble at his back and cause him to flee." However, they marched steadily on. "They were going to look at war, the red animal."

The dragon-army, like the dragon-drink in *George's Mother,* is a comfortable mother-surrogate. With pain and guilt, and yet unspeakable relief, George left his mother to drink with his friends. With much the same mixture of guilt and relief, though the intensity seems much less, Henry left his mother for the army. In the hypothetical sequel to *George's Mother*, George, again with a relief and a feeling of betrayal (perhaps seen in germ when he runs away from the street fight), would have effected the painful rupture with his companions, just as Henry will have to flee in shame from the army, realizing only from his instinctual relief that it was necessary, despite the burden of his guilt, to free himself from this connection, so that he might return to the army as an active and dominant member. Revitalized with the overpowering sense of his individual existence, he would then be able to do battle with that other dragon, which was life outside the maternal sphere.

If *George's Mother* deals mainly with the original separation from the mother, the first part of *The Red Badge* emphasizes this second rupture from the surrogate. At first Henry wants only to maintain his connection with it, but as the crucial moment of battle approaches, he is both less certain of his ability to do so and less convinced of the advisability of doing so. As his doubts grow, the imagery undergoes a shift. Rather than a splendid and unified reptile, the army is split up into superior officers, "mere brutes," who are driving the men into "pens" where they will "all be killed like pigs." From the glittering carnivore, Henry and his fellows are metamorphosed into animals raised for their flesh. But if he were openly to condemn this outrage, he would lose even his fellowship with the other pigs, and become a "worm."

Approaching the fringe of combat, Henry sees more herbivores, a fleeing battalion, a "moblike body of men who galloped like wild horses." The carnivore is now solely on the enemy side, a "composite monster which has caused the other troops to flee." Engaged in his first combat, Henry is without claws or fangs, but "he developed the acute exasperation of a pestered animal, a well-meaning cow worried by dogs," which allowed him to fight creditably, though some of fellows fled "with sheep-like eyes."

But the second assault does for him. The dogs who had worried him have grown into "redoubtable dragons." "At the approach of the red and green monster . . . he seemed to shut his eyes and wait to be gobbled." In terror, seeing one of his companions run "like a rabbit . . . he was like the proverbial chicken." "Directly he began to speed towards the rear with great leaps."

The pattern of imagery reflecting attitude is obvious. In fear, Henry is a rabbit, a horse, cow, sheep, or chicken. The enemy are magical fantastic creatures, monsters, dragons, implacable "machines of steel. It was very gloomy struggling against such affairs, wound up perhaps to fight until sundown."

Fleeing into the woods, Henry tries to find justification for his cowardice in objectifications of his former delusions. A real squirrel runs from danger with a simple logic Henry attempts to equate with his own funk. Obviously, "Nature was of his mind." Conceiving "Nature to be a woman with a deep aversion to tragedy," he conveniently overlooks an ironical intrusion of reality: "He saw, out at some black water, a small animal pounce in and emerge directly with a gleaming fish."

Henry wends his way farther into the calm, distinctly feminine forest, coming at length into the very heart and leafy womb of the woods (described with the same church-like terms as the chapel in *George's Mother* ["He reached a place where the high, arching boughs made a chapel. He softly pushed the green doors aside and entered."]), where with horrible suddenness he is made to confront the peace and security he had been seeking. It is death. "The eyes, staring at the youth, had changed to the dull hue to be seen on the side of a dead fish." Henry, in fleeing from the army, as it was psychologically essential for him to do, had in his terror run backward to an earlier dependency, rather than forward.

In the appalling shock of finding death in the heart of the womb (When George entered his mother's chapel, "far at the end of the room one could discern the pulpit swathed in gloom, solemn and mystic as a bier." Again, at the end of the novel, when, having fled a battle, George returns to his mother, it is to a scene of death. Also, those in the open boat, when separating from one another, at first return to the maternal sea, from which the oiler will not escape alive.), Henry discovers his mistake. Life is outside, then, in the clangor of battle, out where "he conceived two armies to be at each other panther fashion." He runs back to the battle, fleeing from his vision of death as he had before run from what he now realizes to have been the field of life. But the hold of the womb is strong. "Sometimes the brambles formed chains. Trees, confronting him [as parents impeding the progress of infants?], stretched out their arms and forbade him to pass. After its previous hostility its new resistance filled him with a fine bitterness. It seemed that Nature could not be quite ready to kill him." But in fact, she was not quite ready to let him live, as before his mother had been loath to let him go off to battle.

Henry now begins the long painful journey back to life. He must pass through a Dantean inferno of dead and dying, with the secret guilt of knowing he has no right to be among them. These wounded pouring back from the line were innocent victims, sacrificial animals, the Tall Soldier, whose "side looked as if it had been torn by wolves," and the Tattered Man with his "lamb-like eyes." Henry is less than them all, a "worm," a "craven loon."

Through a lucky break, Henry's desertion will not be discovered, for his whole side is being routed. His fellows ran like "terrified buffaloes." "The dragons were coming with invincible strides. The army . . . was going to be swallowed." But Henry has changed. Even in the midst of general terror, he stands apart. His recent profound vision of death has left him eager for life at any cost. The attraction of life, of conflict, which had always worked on him ("He had dreamed of battles . . . of vague and bloody conflicts that had thrilled him with their sweep and fire . . . "), has now gained dominance. "The battle was like the grinding of an immense and terrible machine to him. Its complexities and powers, its grim processes, fascinated him. He must go close and see it produce corpses."

Fear is banished with Henry's new knowledge that no death can match the horror of never having lived. He even inclines to become boyishly scornful, with his new-found courage. Having "been out among dragons . . . he assured himself that they were not so hideous as he had imagined them. Also, they were inaccurate; they did not sting with precision."

In the face of his swelling confidence, the implacable dragons, still deadly, have been demoted to "yelling, eager metallic dogs," and his former fright has turned to anger: " 'Good Gawd,' the youth grumbled, 'we're always being chased around like rats . . . it makes a man feel like a damn kitten in a bag.' " "This advance of the enemy had seemed to the youth like a ruthless hunting," but "he was not going to be badgered out of his life, like a kitten chased by boys, he said. It was not well to drive men into final corners; at these moments they could all develop teeth and claws." In fact, Henry "crouched behind a little tree, with his eyes burning hatefully and his teeth set in a cur-like snarl." The metallic hounds had become "flies sucking insolently at his blood."

Though still retreating, Henry has once more become a carnivore. When the enemy attack falters, he goes "instantly forward, like a dog who, seeing his foes lagging, turns and insists upon being pursued." A moment later his lieutenant says of him, " 'By heavens, if I had ten thousand wild cats like you I could tear th' stomach outa this war in less'n a week!' ''

At last the charge, and Henry and his fellows wrench themselves free of the mother army, and race not to the rear, but headlong into the fray. "This action awakened the men. They huddled no more like sheep." Henry "noted the vicious, wolflike temper of his comrades." He took the regimental flag, the waving, bird-like banner, the "saver of lives," the symbol of salvation, or liberation, which can only be attained with great risk and effort. In "The Open Boat" a man on shore waving his coat offers just such a fluttering symbol; the bird-like brewery in *George's Mother* is another.

The first charge is a failure, and Henry could see the conviction of this "weigh upon the entire regiment until the men were like cuffed and cursed animals, but withal rebellious." They were cast down, but not beaten. They had tasted life, and now, as individuals, came together again as an invincible team.

The sides were once more matched. "It seemed there would shortly be an encounter of strange beaks and claws, as of eagles." The bird image appears again, this time more clearly representing what Erich Neumann, Jung's disciple, has called the "still-primitive fructifying power of the masculine spirit . . . the birds, from the fructifying spirit-doves to Zeus' eagle, [which] are likewise symbols of such spiritual powers, as the rites and myths of all peoples show." The final charge was a success. Snatching at their salvation, "the soldiers had trapped strange birds."

Through our reading of the imagery we have traced the ebb and surge of Henry's courage and confidence as he has been carried along by that rhythm—from sin to redemption, from painful separation to triumphal return—which I have all along been suggesting is central to Crane's major work. I have intimated my belief that this rhythm parallels, at a deeper level, the protagonist's, and perhaps Crane's efforts to become free of an Oedipal fixation. The struggle, in whatever terms one chooses to express it—whether mythical or psychoanalytical—is fundamentally the struggle for individuation, and as such it involves the basic rhythm of all life. At this deepest level of meaning, we discover that the history of Henry's life (ontogeny) has retold the history of life on earth (phylogeny). A re-examination of the imagery shows this clearly.

It is not difficult to see that every detail in the opening lines of *The Red Badge* expresses genesis:

The cold passed reluctantly from the earth, and the retiring fogs revealed an army [the germ of potential life] stretched out on the hills, resting. As the landscape changed from brown to green, the army awakened, and began to tremble with eagerness at the noise of rumours. It cast its eyes upon the roads, which were growing from long troughs of liquid mud to proper thoroughfares.

Day comes, and the army, in prehistoric reptilian guise, sets out in columns "like two serpents crawling from the cavern of night." Early in the novel the images are of great serpents, dragons, giants, or vague monsters moving obscurely in shadows. There follows, as I have already shown in detail, a series of animal transmutations for Henry and the others, extending over the evolutionary spectrum from flies to buffaloes, from worms to wolves. Henry began unformed, simply as a part of the army, "a part of a vast blue demonstration." Later he became a component of a collective monster "wending with many feet." When first a separate animal, he ran with the herd, and had the herd mind. His individual development had its true beginning from the moment he fled the leafy womb in the forest, painfully escaping the fish-eyed corpse, the foetal fish.

After his brief times as a part of a dragon, Henry had been generally, throughout the novel, a docile, driven, preyed-upon beast. But toward the end, his confidence and strength growing, he began to "develop teeth and claws." He became more and more the predator, the dominant animal.

At the end, his animal nature began to pass from him. "Fresh from scenes where many of his usual machines of reflection had been idle, from where he had proceeded sheeplike, he struggled to marshal all his acts." Reflecting, "the youth smiled, for he saw that the world was a world for him . . . he had rid himself of the red sickness of battle. The sultry nightmare was past. He had been an animal blistered and sweating in the heat and pain of war." Now, "he was a man."

Literary Impressionism

James Nagel

In *Active Service,* Crane's longest but least successful novel of war, the narrator reflects that

> perhaps one of the first effects of war upon the mind is a new recognition and fear of the circumscribed ability of the eye, making all landscape seem inscrutable.

This comment is intriguing because it suggests that one of the central concerns of war and, presumably, of fiction about war, is the problem of perception. In a heightened emotional ambience in which accurate interpretation of the environment can determine life or death, there is understandable emphasis on the "circumscribed ability of the eye" and upon any matter that appears "inscrutable." Indeed this rather innocuous remark from *Active Service* suggests a concern for the central narrative method of Crane's finest work, *The Red Badge of Courage.*

The point of view Crane employed in *The Red Badge* is basically that of limited third-person narrator whose access to data is restricted to the mind of the protagonist, Henry Fleming, to his sensory apprehensions and associated thoughts and feelings. In typical Impressionistic manner, Henry's experiences are discontinuous and fragmented and result in a novel composed of brief units. These scenes do not always relate directly to juxtaposed episodes, nor do they always develop the same themes. Furthermore, Henry's view of the battle is severely limited. He knows nothing of the strategy of the battle; he frequently

From *Stephen Crane and Literary Impressionism.* © 1980 by the Pennsylvania State University. Pennsylvania State University Press, 1980.

cannot interpret the events around him because his information is obscured by darkness, smoke, or the noise of cannons; rumors spread quickly throughout his regiment, heightening the fear and anxiety of the men. Often, preoccupied by introspection, Henry's mind distorts the data it receives, transforming men into monsters and artillery shells into shrieking demons that leer at him. In short, Henry's view of things is limited, unreliable, and distorted, and yet a projection of the working of his mind becomes a dramatically realistic depiction of how war might appear to an ordinary private engaged in a battle in the American Civil War.

In an important sense, narrative method is the genious of *The Red Badge*. Of their own, the central events of the novel are commonplace. What gives the novel its unique quality is the method of its telling, its restriction of information. As Orm Överland has pointed out,

> throughout *The Red Badge* (except in the first paragraph where, as it were, the "camera eye" settles down on the camp and the youth, and the concluding one where it again recedes) we in our imagined roles as spectators never have a larger view of the field than has the main character.

Many other Crane scholars have commented on this technique, and most of them invoke a visual metaphor, such as the "camera eye," to describe the method. Carl Van Doren, for example, wrote in the *American Mercury* in 1924 that Henry Fleming "is a lens through which a whole battle may be seen, a sensorium upon which all its details may be registered." Although Van Doren is overgenerous in his analysis of how much of the battle Henry actually sees, he is essentially correct in classifying the methodology of its rendition. Indeed, even thirty years after its initial publication, *The Red Badge* must have seemed most remarkable, for no third-person novel in American literature previously published had so severely limited its point of view. That such restriction is Impressionistic has been well established by Sergio Perosa:

> *The Red Badge of Courage* is indeed a triumph of impressionistic vision and impressionistic technique. Only a few episodes are described from the outside; Fleming's mind is seldom analyzed in an objective, omniscient way; very few incidents are extensively *told*. Practically every scene is filtered through Fleming's point of view and seen through his eyes. Everything is related to his *vision,* to his *sense*-perception of

incidents and details, to his *sense*-reactions rather than to his psychological impulses, to his confused sensations and individual impressions.

There is somewhat more "telling" by the narrator than Perosa's comment suggests, and perhaps more interplay from Henry's "psychological impulses," but this formulation of the narrative method of the novel is essentially accurate. Although there are a few passages with an intrusive narrative presence, and a few other complicating devices involving temporal dislocations, the central device of the novel is the rendering of action and thought as they occur in Henry's mind, revealing not the whole of the battle, nor even the broad significance of it, but rather the meaning of this experience to him. The immediacy of the dramatic action is a product of the rendering of the sensory data of Henry's mind; the psychological penetration results from the mingling of experience with association, distortion, fantasy, and memory. A further implication of this method, one that is unsettling but realistic, is that the world presented to Henry is beyond his control, beyond even his comprehension. His primary relation to it is not so much a matter of his deeds as of his organization of sensation into language and pattern.

No reading of *The Red Badge of Courage* can be complete, therefore, which does not deal with the significance of perception in the novel as both a methodological and thematic component. In this sense, the method of the novel is a rendering of Fleming's apprehension and his thoughts: its unifying and informing theme is the development of his capacity to *see* himself, in the context of war, more clearly. Henry's initiation into a nominal maturity becomes a function of his perception of life, death, and his own consuming, nearly incapacitating, fear. After the opening of the novel, the concentration is on Henry's mind. In the first paragraph, however, before Henry has been introduced, an abstract, third-person narrator presents an establishing scene:

> The cold passed reluctantly from the earth and the retiring fogs revealed an army stretched out on the hills, resting. As the landscape changed from brown to green the army awakened and began to tremble with eagerness at the noise of rumors. It cast its eyes upon the roads which were growing from long troughs of liquid mud to proper thoroughfares. A river, amber-tinted in the shadow of its banks, purled at the army's feet and at night when the stream had become

> of a sorrowful blackness one could see, across, the red eye-like gleam of hostile camp-fires set in the low brows of distant hills.

This paragraph contains not only objective descriptive details but a subjective and animating quality as well. The cold retreats "reluctantly," suggesting a desire to remain, to the discomfort of the soldiers; the fog which has obscured the scene, now "reveals" the Union army in the hills; the army, personified into a composite and singular entity, "trembles" in response to rumors and casts its "eyes" across the scene. It is an opening filled with tension and ominous suggestion. As J. C. Levenson has pointed out, "the reader enters an animistic scene in which red eyes gleam beneath the low brows of hills and the whole world of consciousness is alive and active and menacing." The characters, introduced in terms of their sensory indicators (the tall soldier, the loud soldier, the youth) to a narrative mind free of prior knowledge, behave nervously. Thus the opening ambience establishes the tone as well as the topography of the novel.

As soon as Henry Fleming is introduced, the center of intelligence becomes his: "There was a youthful private who listened with eager ears to the words of the tall soldier and to the varied comments of his comrades." From this point on, the central concern of the novel is the literal and figurative dimensions of his perception. The most obvious examples of this mode are narrative assertions about Henry's eyes and what he can see. The thrust of the novel is on Henry's mind rather than on the battle itself, and these comments are essentially revelations of character. For example, several passages reveal his egotistic conception of his superior vision, as when he concludes that "there was but one pair of eyes in the corps," or when, after his desertion, he feels that the limitations of his comrades "would not enable them to understand his sharper point of view." Of greater thematic significance are those passages which relate knowledge in terms of vision, as when Henry realizes that Wilson has changed from a "loud young soldier" to one of quiet confidence:

> The youth wondered where had been born these new eyes; when his comrade had made the great discovery that there were many men who would refuse to be subjected by him. Apparently, the other had now climbed a peak of wisdom from which he could perceive himself as a very wee thing.

Significantly, Wilson's development of insight, of true self-knowledge, precedes Henry's. Wilson, who functions in some ways as Henry's alter-ego in the second half of the novel, has experienced his perceptual initiation by chapter 14; Henry's does not come until chapter 18, at which point it is formulated in terms of a similar visual metaphor:

> These happenings had occupied an incredibly short time yet the youth felt that in them he had been made aged. New eyes were given to him. And the most startling thing was to learn suddenly that he was very insignificant.

For Henry, this passage had a function beyond its metaphoric value. For the first time he is able to see clearly:

> It seemed to the youth that he saw everything. Each blade of the green grass was bold and clear. He thought that he was aware of every change in the thin, transparent vapor that floated idly in sheets.

The psychological implication of Henry's transformation is that his preoccupation with fear, and his projection of heroic stature for his brave deeds, had obscured reality and prevented him from seeing himself in context. Now that he sees himself as one with his fellows, as an individual no more significant than any other, within the impersonal machinations of war, he develops the capacity to comprehend his environment: "His mind took mechanical but firm impressions, so that, afterward, everything was pictured and explained to him, save why he himself was there." The conclusion of the novel, which marks a juncture not in the battle but in Henry's development, continues the concentration on vision. In the final scene, Henry's "eyes seemed to open to some new ways. He found that he could look back upon the brass and bombast of his earlier gospels and see them truly." In visual terms, there is no doubt that Henry has undergone significant development: he has relinquished his dreams of "Greek-like struggles" as well as his fear, which had become "the red sickness of battle," in favor of a more mature and balanced picture of himself as part of humanity.

As might be expected from the narrative stance of the novel, there is a stress on the sensory faculties. The reader, like the viewer of an Impressionistic painting, is presented with an array of sensational details from a scene: the colors, sounds, feelings of a given experience. In chapter 3, for example, after a visual passage in which Henry keeps "his eyes watchfully upon the darkness," other senses come into play: the smell of the pines is pervasive; the sounds of insects and axes echo through the forest; and Henry's sensations of touch become acute:

> His canteen banged rhythmically upon his thigh and his haversack bobbed softly. His musket bounced a trifle from his shoulder at each stride and made his cap feel uncertain upon his head.

But the predominant sensory emphasis is on vision, so much so that Harold Frederic, himself a skilled novelist, called *The Red Badge* a "battle painting" in his review in the New York *Times* in 1896. Sensitive to Crane's narrative method, Frederic remarked that as readers "we see with his [Henry's] eyes, think with his mind, quail or thrill with his nerve." Frederic concluded that this method of "photographic revelation" accounts for the fascination of the novel. Frederic's comments have more than figurative significance, for there is a good deal of narrative "picturing." One expression of this device is subjective, generated within Henry's mind, as in the opening chapter: "His busy mind had drawn for him large pictures, extravagant in color, lurid with breathless deeds." The method is essentially expository, evoking no coordinate image but rather a generic sense of the workings of Henry's mind. Paradoxically, most of the passages labeled pictures by the narrator constitute internal rather than external renderings. In general, when Henry is confused and under stress, his mind seeks resolution through imaginative portraits. One such instance occurs in chapter 11, in which Henry, filled with guilt for his desertion and remorse for the death of Jim Conklin, sees "swift pictures of himself, apart, yet in himself." The first image he conjures is of himself in a heroic moment of death, standing bravely, "getting calmly killed on a high place before the eyes of all." He imagines as well the "magnificent pathos of his dead body." This image temporarily expiates his sense of shame and for a few moments "he was sublime." He constructs a more sustaining image of himself at the front of battle, then loses confidence in his capacity for heroic action. Thus one function of narrative picturing is the projection of Henry's internal fantasy, creating visual correlatives for his heroic striving and compensatory fears of cowardice and death. So it is with Henry's "visions" and "pictures" in the opening chapter and his "dreams" throughout the novel.

To some extent, Henry is forced to imaginative picturing to find coherence and unity in his experience, for his sensory data is confused and incomplete. During the battle in which he deserts, smoke blankets the battlefield, as it does often, and allows him only "changing views" of the action. One of his central problems throughout the novel is that he cannot perceive enough to construct a reliable interpretation of his situation: his comrades appear to him as "dark waves" and the enemy as "grey shadows" in the woods. A "clouded haze" obscures almost every important scene. In the absence of congruent information about the events, Henry's mind interprets the limited data in terms of his fear. He never has access to all he would like to see:

> The youth leaned his breast against the brown dirt and peered over at the woods and up and down the line. Curtains of trees interfered with his ways of vision. He could see the low line of trenches but for a short distance.

In another scene, in which Henry is so close to the rebel troops that he can momentarily distinguish the features of individual men, his view is changed before he can act:

> Almost instantly, they [the Southern troops] were shut utterly from the youth's sight by the smoke from the energetic rifles of his companions. He strained his vision to learn the accomplishment of the volley but the smoke hung before him.

It is clear throughout the novel that given limited information, Henry must struggle to understand his circumstances. After one battle, in which it seemed to him that he had covered a great deal of ground, he has an opportunity to survey what has actually happened: "He discovered that the distances, as compared with the brilliant measurings of his mind, were trivial and ridiculous."

In most cases, however, Henry is not allowed to reflect upon the accuracy of his interpretations, and his fears and visions distort the data he receives. The most dramatic of these instances come during battle, and most of them involve Henry's perception of battle objects as dragons and monsters of various kinds. The first such image exemplifies his distortions: "From off in the darkness, came the trampling of feet. The youth could occasionally see dark shadows that moved like monsters." When he next peers across the river at the enemy camp fires, he sees them as "growing larger, as the orbs of a row of dragons, advancing." Even when his own regiment moves through the darkness the men appear to be "monsters" which strike Henry as "huge crawling reptiles." As a result, the early part of the novel is filled with "serpents," "monsters," "battle-phantoms," "dragons," and other fantastic manifestations of "war, the red animal, war, the blood-swollen god." Significantly, Henry's distortions are consistent until chapter 18, when he experiences a dramatic epiphany and "new eyes were given to him." Previously he had been capable of almost surrealistic projections, as when he imagines that the artillery shells arching over him have "rows of cruel teeth that grinned at him," or later, when coming upon some of his comrades in the forest,

> his disordered mind interpreted the hall of the forest as a charnel place. He believed for an instant that he was in the house of the dead and he did not dare to move lest these corpses start up, squalling and squawking.

After his moment of recognition, in which he perceives his insignificance and loses much of his fear, there are no such distortions. It is then that he can see his earlier errors of interpretation: "Elfin thoughts must have exaggerated and enlarged everything, he said." He is still subject to sensory restriction and obscuring, as when a scene becomes a "wild blur" as he dashes across a field, but he no longer creates monsters out of shadows.

Indeed much of the narrative emphasis is on his improved capacity to perceive:

> His vision being unmolested by smoke from the rifles of his companions, he had opportunities to see parts of the hard fight. It was a relief to perceive at last from whence came some of these noises which had been roared into his ears.

As the narrator makes explicit, Henry's new sight is more than a literal clarity of apprehension; it involves cognitive factors as well. In the final chapter,

> gradually his brain emerged from the clogged clouds and at last he was enabled to more closely comprehend himself and circumstance. . . . He understood then that the existence of shot and counter-shot was in the past. . . . Later, he began to study his deeds—his failures and his achievements. . . . At last, they marched before him clearly. From this present view-point, he was enabled to look upon them in spectator fashion and to criticise them with some correctness.

The novel concludes with a visual emphasis. As Henry's "eyes seemed to open to some new ways," he is able to reflect on his earlier ideas and "sees them truly."

In an important sense, *The Red Badge* is a novel of the growth of Henry's visual capacities. The narrative method, alternating from objective apprehensions presented in the manner of a motion picture camera to the subjective rendering of his distortions, emotions, fantasies, and memories, is the single most innovative device in the novel. As J. C. Levenson has commended, Crane's

> radical breakthrough came from his premise that mental life primarily consists in witnessing the vivid immediate presences within one's own mind, that is, in the flux of consciousness. So far as consciousness is concerned, self-projected images have equal status with sense data.

For Henry Fleming these "self-projected images" consist of both evocations generated out of internal need and interpretative distortions of genuine sensory data, and he is largely unable to distinguish between them.

Beyond these narrative methodologies, which dominate the novel, there are several other strategies that play a role in individual scenes. If the flashback technique can be theoretically reconciled with Impressionism in fiction as a narrative projection of thought, it is more difficult to establish congruence with Impressionism of moments that jump forward, even if they present a future, retrospective time: "When he thought of it later, he conceived the impression that it is better to view the appalling than to be merely within hearing." It is even more difficult to understand intrusive passages as part of an Impressionistic novel, and there are a few of them in *The Red Badge*. One such passage occurs in chapter 3: "But the regiment was not yet veteran-like in appearance. Veteran regiments in this army were likely to be very small aggregations of men." It seems unlikely that this comment can be read as the narrator's statement of Henry's thoughts since he is a raw recruit who has yet to see his first battle and knows little of the size of battle-torn regiments. The later image of "guns squatted in a row like savage chiefs" again seems to derive from beyond Henry's frame of reference. But such passages are rare and do not substantially qualify the Impressionistic method that dominates the novel. It should be noted, however, that there is more variation of narrative logic than has generally been acknowledged. There is even one passage of direct thought as in stream of consciousness: "The youth pitied them [a group of artillery gunners] as he ran. Methodical idiots! Machine-like fools!" Here, in an intensely emotional moment, the intervening narrative consciousness disappears to render Henry's thoughts precisely as they occur.

Despite these variations, the basic method of the "showing" of *The Red Badge of Courage* is Impressionistic and consists of the sensations and thoughts of a private engaged in a battle he does not comprehend and cannot even clearly see. The drama of the novel is epistemological, a matter of perception, distortion, and realization which finally culminates in chapter 18 with Henry's epiphany. The genius of the novel is its use of a narrative method that underscores the perceptual themes, that forces the reader to participate in the empirical limitations of the central character, and that creates a psychological reality on a level never before achieved in the American novel.

Stephen Crane: The Hero as Victim

Harold Beaver

> *We picture the world as thick with conquering and elate humanity, but here, with the bugles of the tempest pealing, it was hard to imagine a peopled earth. One viewed the existence of man then as a marvel, and conceded a glamor of wonder to these lice, which were caused to cling to a whirling, fire-smote, ice-locked, disease-stricken, space-lost bulb. The conceit of man was explained by this storm to be the very engine of life.*
>
> —*The Blue Hotel*, chapter 8

By the late nineteenth century the heroic ideal, though noisily encouraged in romantic fiction and by the popular press, had become harder and harder to sustain. For the myth of heroism was dependent upon free will. But what Mendel and Ricardo and Marx and Darwin and Freud and Malthus had seemingly taught was that man was trapped; that he was the unsuspecting victim of genetic and economic and political and evolutionary and psychological forces, including an ever-spiralling population growth. The myth of heroism, moreover, depended on a vision of an integrated society with its own economic and sexual hierarchies, its own natural and supernatural controls. But, by the end of the century, the whole universe, it seemed, had disintegrated into a chaos of competing and anarchic forces, receding ever faster to a state of entropic collapse. Such forces, by definition, were beyond human control. No counterattack, however defiant, could be waged by an individual alone.

By collective action, perhaps: "The mode of production of material

From *The Yearbook of English Studies* 12 (1982). © 1982 by Modern Humanities Research Association.

life," Marx had written in his preface to *The Critique of Political Economy,* "conditions the general process of social, political and intellectual life." Or, as the American Henry George put it, "the idea that man mentally and physically is the result of slow modifications, perpetuated by heredity, irresistibly suggests the idea that it is the race life, not the individual life, which is the object of human existence." Such was the gospel of *Progress and Poverty* (1879). But the authorship of books was hardly ever collective; it was indifferent to progress; and by the late nineteenth century had become even more intuned, if anything, to in-dividual "human existence." The overriding task remained, as always, one of composition. That alone, in a decomposing universe, made the writer's role potentially heroic.

Stephen Crane was among the most self-conscious of this new breed of heroic writers. Henry Adams, his fellow American, chose to confront the *intellectual* responsibility of opting for anarchy. Crane chose to confront the *moral* responsibility (amid "the bugles of the tempest pealing") of reeling through the blizzard. For it was as if a blizzard had struck the old American certainties. The new forces of Hegelian idealism and Darwinian biology and economic determinism—of evolu-tion, class warfare, and heredity—were peculiarly stacked against the old Jeffersonian belief in personal self-control. Romantic individualism quickly soured, in the decades after the Civil War, to a documentary pessimism. Even before 1860 a brilliant minority of American writers, which included Hawthorne and Melville, had opted for pessimism. But now there were mass deserters. By 1900 the cleft between high art and "pop" art was complete. It opened a chasm between serious fiction and fun, or escapist uplift, in western and athletic "profiles" of which we are the inevitable heirs. For it was in this generation that the moral rewards of capitalism were first subverted; that Horatio Alger's call of "rags to riches," "Log Cabin to White House," was finally undercut by the new Naturalist Novel. The hero of self-improvement, U.S.-style, was shown, for good or ill, to be a mere victim of cir-cumstances and/or his own illusions.

One native response was to ask: "So what?" "What, in short," in the words of William James, "is the truth's cash value in experiential terms?" But pragmatism was of little use to men who felt already doomed; for whom both Christianity and the promise of the Greek Revival had failed; who felt excluded from both the old religious and the Homeric appeals to personal glory. Like Dante, the young Stephen Crane awoke to find all confused, all lost. "He had long despaired of witnessing a Greeklike struggle." He aimed to fight his way out of that modern *selva oscura,* or Darwinian jungle. *The Red Badge of Courage* was to be his report from the jungle.

It appeared in 1895, a year after Kipling's *The Jungle Book,* four years before Conrad's *Heart of Darkness.* Crane was still only twenty-four years old. His subject was that of the hunters and the hunted, of the predators and the victims (much as that of Joel Chandler Harris's *Uncle Remus* tales) in a savagely destructive world. But his literary talent lay far from vernacular or folk tale. It comprised, above all, a split-second markmanship in stalking his prey, nicknamed by contemporary photojournalists the "snapshot." This new heroic style was to rival Homer's for clarity. This new American *Iliad,* too, was subdivided into twenty-four parts. Had not the war, which it commemorated, been won by Ulysses S. Grant? Had not the artist, who first commemorated it, himself been called Winslow Homer? Like that American Homer's, Crane's theme was to be read as neither the romance of heroism, nor the triumph of heroism, but the quandary of heroism in an unheroic age, or rather (to use the title of one of his own later stories) the "Mystery of Heroism."

For the Darwinian metaphor, red in tooth and claw, had been miraculously turned inside out on that battlefield to become a scenario for this "naturalist," or reportage-like, fiction. Here Crane could study the human condition, in all its turbulence, with the most exacting details of historical research. In this, too, he proved himself to be profoundly American. However realistic his setting, or his tone, he was still writing "romances," like his great contemporary, Henry James. What Puritan New England had been for Hawthorne, the Virginian landscape of the Civil War was to be for Crane. Instead of the meeting-houses and the custom-houses, the colonial wilderness and the Indians of the North, he would present the pine barrens, in mist and gunsmoke, of the South. Instead of a *Scarlet Letter,* he would depict a *Red Badge* of shame. Only the meaning shifts. Hawthorne's "letters of guilt" would here turn to "red letters of curious revenge." For the theme was no longer that of lust, or some Faustian perusal of sin on a black-and-white frontier, but the psychological backlash of fear.

Just as Hawthorne, furthermore, had studied John Mason and William Hubbard and Cotton and Increase Mather (his seventeenth-century sources for the Indian Wars), so Crane poured over the *Battles and Leaders of the Civil War,* Harper's *History,* the drawings of Winslow Homer, and the photographs of Mathew Brady. Their battle scenes became for him a kind of ritual test, a crisis of identity even. He had missed the Great War. He belonged to a post-war generation, guiltily hankering for some extreme engagement in a commercial and prosaic age. He studied the plans of the attacks and counterattacks of the battle of Chancellorsville (May 2–4, 1863). He mentally reconstructed that wilderness, ten miles west of Fredericksburg on the Rappahannock River, in which Sedgwick and Hooker were forced back across the river by Lee's bluff, and the brilliant fifteen-mile flanking attack, in which Stonewall Jackson was mortally wounded. This was Lee's last great victory, leading to his invasion of the North in the Gettysburg Campaign. It becomes the visual and tactical source for *The Red Badge of Courage.*

For the fictional exercise came first. The emotional rehearsal came first. As with young writers, Crane's career seems curiously inverted, though what began as a purely literary experience eventually took him to Mexico, and to Cuba and Greece to cover the Turkish War as a war correspondent. Later, when he came to write *The Open Boat,* his text recreated the context of his own life. But when he wrote *The Red Badge of Courage* his text had to follow another's text. It was from Stendhal's *Le Rouge et le Noir,* from Tolstoy's *Sevastopol Sketches* and the great Borodino scenes, as viewed by Pierre in *War and Peace,* that Crane learnt to use his single incoherent angle of vision. For the confusion of soldiers and cavalry charges, the roar of guns and the crackle of rifles, the whole mad inconsequence of war were for Crane hugely symbolic of all terror, all uncertainty, all ultimate loneliness. Everything is questioned: the battle, the wound, the heroism, the resolution and self-respect reassembled out of doubts and lies. Crane's Chancellorsville is revealed as a cosmic trap, an absurd non-event. In the final chapter, the regiment finds itself winding back to the river it had originally crossed a few days earlier, as if nothing had happened.

For nothing, in a sense, had happened. Nothing ever happens. Everything becomes part of the antics of non-communication, which was to become Crane's final symbol (in *The Open Boat)* for the existential void in which his actors prate and strut and cower and flee; and sometimes survive; and sometimes face death with steady dignity and calm. Battle lust is directly compared to mad religion; the Civil War, to a sectarian conflict—as if fought by lapsed Methodists to the tune of:

> Fight the good fight with all thy might,
> Christ is thy strength, and Christ thy right;

Lay hold on life, and it shall be
Thy joy and crown eternally . . .

Faint not nor fear. His arms are near,
He changeth not, and thou art dear;
Only believe, and thou shalt see
That Christ is all in all to thee.

"Well, God reigns, and in his hands we are safe, whatever awaits us,"
was his father's habitual refrain. Again and again (in *Maggie,* in *George's
Mother,* in *The Blue Hotel,* in *The Bride Comes to Yellow Sky*) Stephen Crane
seems to confront his father's snug Methodism, while simultaneously
questioning the American demand for aggression, the American pride
in the predatory toughguy, the Bowery kid with patent-leather shoes
"like weapons," or Westerners with guns on their hips. The attack is
two-pronged.

For *The Red Badge of Courage* is charged with religious imagery:
the *Ecce Homo* of the "dead man who was seated with his back against
a columnlike tree"; the notorious red sun "pasted in the sky like a wafer."
Yet the communion of modern warfare proves a camaraderie of the
absurd. The sacrifice of John Conklin (another J. C.) turns to a pointless
danse-macabre, like the "devotee of a mad religion, blood-sucking,
muscle-wrenching, bone-crushing." The red badge of courage itself
proves to be panic-stricken and self-inflicted. Self-discovery and personal salvation turn out inevitably to be a patched lie in a meaningless
war. Even to bear the colours, that sacred trust, is merely to feel "the
daring spirit of a savage religion-mad." All attempts to shape a moral
vision are ultimately reduced to madness in an amoral universe. For
"secular and religious education had" by no means "effaced the throat-
grappling instinct," nor "firm finance held in check the passions." From
Crane's desperate vision runs a direct line to Hemingway's nihilist
litanies.

H. G. Wells was right when he wrote that Crane's writings suggested not so much Tolstoy, or Conrad's *Lord Jim,* as Whistler. Wells
praised him for his "impressionism." We might prefer to use "expres-
sionism" for those suns and wounds entangled in a single obsession,
like Van Gogh's *Sunflowers,* or Edvard Munch's *The Scream.* Brown,
red, yellow, blue, grey, green, are laid on with a pointilliste discretion,
learnt from the emotive spectrum of Goethe's *Colour Lore.* Even in his
titles: *The Red Badge of Courage; The Black Riders; The Blue Hotel; The*

Bride Comes to Yellow Sky. His snapshot vision has the terrible, often hallucinatory, clarity of dream:

> Once he found himself almost into a swamp. He was oblig-ed to walk upon bog tufts and watch his feet to keep from the oily mire. Pausing at one time to look about him he saw, out at some black water, a small animal pounce in and emerge directly with a gleaming fish.
>
> The youth went again into the deep thickets. The brushed branches made a noise that drowned the sound of cannon. He walked on, going from obscurity into promises of a greater obscurity.
>
> At length he reached a place where the high, arching boughs made a chapel. He softly pushed the green doors aside and entered. Pine needles were a gentle brown carpet. There was a religious half light.
>
> Near the threshold he stopped, horror-stricken at the sight of a thing.
>
> He was being looked at by a dead man who was seated with his back against a columnlike tree. The corpse was dressed in a uniform that once had been blue, but was now faded to a melancholy shade of green. The eyes, staring at the youth, had changed to the dull hue to be seen on the side of a dead fish. The mouth was open. Its red had chang-ed to an appalling yellow. Over the gray skin of the face ran little ants. One was trundling some sort of a bundle along the upper lip.
>
> (*The Red Badge of Courage,* chapter 7)

Concentrate. Focus. Advance. After the "pounce," a "trundling": and the "gleaming fish" reemerges a "dead fish," while those primary reds and blues are dissolved, in alliteration, to a foggy yellow and pervasive green.

Such shifts of mood and their ironies constitute the pattern of Crane's work. Though capable of explication, like the symbolism of Van Gogh's canvases, they ultimately resist—must resist—a reductive interpretation into patterns of mortal and spiritual significance. In this Crane is not like Hawthorne, nor fundamentally, I think, like Melville. Henry Fleming ("the youth" of *The Red Badge of Courage*) can never be wholly educated out of his illusions, his fantasies, his flickering shifts of mood. Crane did his best to impose an ending:

Yet gradually he mustered force to put the sin at a distance. And at last his eyes seemed to open to some new ways. He found that he could look back upon the brass and bombast of his earlier gospels and see them truly. He was gleeful when he discovered that he now despised them.

With the conviction came a store of assurance. He felt a quiet manhood, nonassertive but of sturdy and strong blood. He knew that he would no more quail before his guides wherever they should point. He had been to touch the great death, and found that, after all, it was but the great death. He was a man.

(*The Red Badge of Courage,* chapter 24)

But that seems rather pretentious, strained. He tried rewriting it several times. For just as Henry had fled from battle, in pursuit of a squirrel skittering into the trees, so the blind rage that turns him into a hero, a flag-bearer in the end, is mere animal rage. Man is out of control: that is the burden of Crane's message. Far from reason or courage, it is illusion and impulse, again and again, that twiches and throws us.

The Red Badge of Courage reads like some zany inscrutable allegory of *non-sense.* Crane's soldiers are seldom named: "the youth" (Henry Fleming), the "tall soldier" (Jim Conklin), the "loud soldier" (Wilson), the "spectral soldier," the "tattered man," the man with a "cheery voice," the man with a shoeful of blood who "hopped like a schoolboy in a game," who "was laughing hysterically." A decade earlier, in *Specimen Days,* Whitman had written of the unknown dead, "The Million Dead."

(In some of the cemeteries nearly *all* the dead are unknown. At Salisbury, N.C., for instance, the known are only 85, while the unknown are 12,027, and 11,700 of these are buried in trenches. A national monument has been put up here, by order of Congress, to mark the spot—but what visible, material monument can ever fittingly commemorate that spot?)

It was Crane who composed that "visible, material monument." Long before the multiplication of Tombs of Unknown Warriors throughout the world, Crane had revealed that warrior, with his schoolboy hop and hysterical laugh, as the scared and impotent victim. Long before Wilfred Owen and Siegfried Sassoon, Crane had confronted the chauvinism, the imperialism, the patriotic humbug of a bellicose decade that gloried in the honour and self-sacrifice of war. In modern wars, he taught, it is the victims who are greeted as heroes.

For death, he realized, *exposes* man. It is the final betrayal of lives mercifully protected by shame, concealment, lies. Like the paper-thin torn soles of the shoes on the feet of a fallen soldier: "it was as if fate had betrayed the soldier. In death it exposed to his enemies that poverty which in life he had perhaps concealed from his friends." Wounds, however, may strangely glorify a man. As he declared in "An Episode of War":

> A wound gives strange dignity to him who bears it. Well men shy from his new and terrible majesty. It is as if the wounded man's hand is upon the curtain which hangs before the revelations of all existence—the meaning of ants, poten-tates, wars, cities, sunshine, snow, a feather dropped from a bird's wing; and the power of it sheds radiance upon a bloody form, and makes the other men understand some-times that they are little.

Crane himself, throughout his short career, seems a wounded man, a suicidally haunted man, in his far-ranging quest for wars from Cuba to Turkey. At the time of writing *The Red Badge of Courage* he had come no closer to war than Philoctetes. Like Hemingway, his heir, he seems a ready-made case-book study for Edmund Wilson's *The Wound and the Bow*. All his fiction, whether set in the Bowery or in the Virginian or Western wilds, seems to fashion his own psychological skirmish, in tougher and tougher engagements, with the amoral, aggressive, com-mercial, bourgeois jungle of the 1890s.

How does one plot a meaningful life? How plot a meaningful life in such a meaningless universe? Man cannot be wholly predetermined, he seems to say. Economic and social and hereditary environment can-not be all. Men *must* be seen as first movers. Men *must* retain the illu-sion of free will, to operate in spite of their environment. Against the sins of pride and self-delusion, the sycophantic faith in society's codes and the dogmas of God, must be asserted the moral responsibility of self-definition. "In a story of mine called 'An Experiment in Misery,' " he wrote, "I tried to make plain that the root of Bowery life is a sort of cowardice. Perhaps I mean a lack of ambition or to wil-lingly be knocked flat and accept the licking." Crane viewed the bums of the Bowery flophouses uncompromisingly. Cowards are those who cannot confront the question of self-definition. Heroes can and do.

Cowards are those who fall prey to social delusions, from whom Crane abdicates all responsibility as a writer. Cowards are those who fail to stand up against the "collaboration of sin," like the Easterner in tacit alliance with the card-sharper (of *The Blue Hotel*) versus an outsider. The iron bars of tradition and of the law in which man travels Crane called "a moving box." The problem is that of living without bars, without order, outside dogmas or codes, in a blizzard of whirling and competing forces. The question is one of decomposition with dignity in a decomposing universe. Not only the roles but the writing must be disintegrated to reassert our inherent worth and dignity as men.

The ultimate question is that of heroism: not the passionate heroism of Crane's pseudo-heroes—rushing to save, to kill, to prop the flag—but the stoic restraint of a Jim Conklin (in *The Red Badge of Courage*) or the correspondent (in *The Open Boat*). Neither the Swede fuelled on Scully's whisky (in *The Blue Hotel*), nor black Henry Johnson rushing into a blazing laboratory (in *The Monster*), nor Fred Collins recklessly crossing noman's land for some water (in "A Mystery of Heroism"), nor Henry Fleming in his final berserker fury, is a hero. All are "blindly led by quaint emotions." All, even at best, are masters merely of their own visionary worlds. As Emily Dickinson once put it:

> A coward will remain, Sir,
> Until the fight is done;
> But an *immortal hero*
> Will take his hat, and run!

True heroes act with a nervous integrity: "as deliberate and exact as so many watchmakers," as Crane wrote of the Cuban conflict. In his final writings (in "The Veteran," "The Price of the Harness," *Wounds in the Rain,* the Spitzbergen tales) Crane dealt increasingly with such cool deliberation. Theirs is the dignity of self-possession. Heroes are those who can go forward, alone; who accept moral responsibility for themselves and others; who can accept isolation; who remain committed to life; who stand up to the "collaboration of sin." Though they too, of course, must die. They too, like Jim Conklin, may at any moment collapse with an animal-like kick of death.

Crane's heroes cradle their wounds in careful self-support, grabbing their left arm with their right hand, or holding their right wrist tenderly as if it were "made of very brittle glass." For Crane saw through the dignity to the fragility and the pathos of self-possession. He was still only twenty-eight years old when he died. It was of tuberculosis that he died. Within a generation his fragile dignity was reduced to a mere code, a moral shorthand for stoic self-definition and self-control. That is often called Hemingway's code.

Yet Hemingway also delivered Crane's finest epitaph. "What about the good writers," asks a German in *Green Hills of Africa*. "The good writers are Henry James, Stephen Crane and Mark Twain," Hemingway replies. "That's not the order they're good in. There is no order for good writers." And what happened to Crane? the German asks. "He died. That's simple. He was dying from the start."

Fear, Rage, and the Mistrials
of Representation
in *The Red Badge of Courage*

Donald Pease

In the April 1896 issue of *The Dial,* Army General A. C. McClurg, in a critical document interesting less for the general's insight into the novel than the direction of his criticism of it, bitterly denounced *The Red Badge of Courage* as a vicious satire of army life. "The hero of the book, if such he can be called, was an ignorant and stupid country lad without a spark of patriotic feeling or soldierly ambition," the general wrote. "He is throughout an idiot or a maniac and betrays no trace of the reasoning being. No thrill of patriotic devotion to cause or country ever moves his breast, and not even an emotion of manly courage." And after noting the work is that of a young man, and therefore must be a mere work of "diseased imagination," the general concludes, in a catalogue informed with political as well as dramatic principles, that "Soldier Fleming is a coward, a Northerner who fled the field . . . and that is why the British have praised *The Red Badge."* Suspending for a moment any question of the accuracy in the general's remarks, we cannot fail to register the force in his reaction. Nor can we fail to notice the source of the general's rage: the absence in Private Fleming's account of those virtues usually included in conventional war narratives whenever describing or justifying the excesses of war. Moreover, although the general does not explicitly mention it, his reaction to still another omission proves clear enough from the fury in

From *American Realism: New Essays,* edited by Eric J. Sundquist. © 1982 by The Johns Hopkins University Press.

his final barrage of accusations. That Crane would represent battle conditions frightening enough to produce cowards might perhaps be excusable, but that he would present such conditions in a context devoid of such crucial issues as the slavery question or southern secession, issues bound to inspire in the reader what they failed to evoke from Private Fleming, namely a renewed commitment to the Union cause, must in General McClurg's mind be grounds for the charge of treason.

Clearly Crane inflamed the general's ire by leaving political considerations out of his account altogether. Written at a time when the nation's historians were characterizing the political and ideological significance of seemingly every battle in the war, Crane's power derived from his decision to reverse the procedure. By stripping the names from the battles he describes, Crane releases the sheer force of the battle incidents unrelieved by their assimilation into a historical narrative frame. And like a naive social historian, General McClurg decided to make good on the debits in Crane's account. In his critical relation to the war novel he restored to the narrative what Crane carefully eliminated from Henry Fleming's confrontation with war: a political and moral frame of reference.

By 1896, many American historians considered the Civil War the decisive moment in the nation's "coming of age." A moment's reflection on the contentions in early documentary accounts of the war should indicate the crucial role it played in providing a young nation with both a historical and a geographical orientation. For many historians viewed this war as a struggle that cross-identified ideological and geographical demarcations and finally granted a name and a sense of place to the United States of America. Given their evaluation of the crucial role the war played in the formation of national character, it was difficult if not impossible to eliminate moral questions from their accounts of the war. While few historians argued that freedom, equality, and union were decisively secured in the aftermath to the war, none denied the ideological power of these abstract principles. Indeed the moral values inherent in these principles not only affected these accounts, in some accounts they replaced battle descriptions altogether.

While Civil War narratives had developed into a flourishing enterprise capable of deflecting all considerations of the experience of the war into an ideological frame of reference intent on justifying it, Crane in registering the effects of the war innocent of the consolations of any coherent ground whatever defied the captains of the war industry. Once we acknowledge the number of reviews and critical studies that have either overlooked or scrupulously read back into *The Red Badge of Courage* what Crane has carefully eliminated, no further evidence of the pervasive hold of the typical Civil War narrative wields over the American imagination need be mentioned. What needs reiteration, however, is the threat not only against the Civil War industry but against America as a nation implicit in Crane's narrative. For if the conventional war narrative used the Civil War as a pretext for an ideological recounting of those principles that gave shape to a nation, Crane, by excluding these principles, was guilty of an assault against the American character. To register the force of this attack, however, we must read Crane through the eyes of a military officer eager to order a young nation to shape up, to conform to the features of stability and confidence delineated and secured by the war. General McClurg in his review, then, did not wish to launch a personal attack on Private Fleming but to recover those representations Stephen Crane had withheld. As the general's review vividly attests, by 1896 these representations had become ingrained enough in the American character for one of her "representative men" to take their absence as a personal affront.

By mentioning General McClurg's reaction specifically, I do not mean to isolate its eccentricity, but to suggest that in its very force his reaction represents the urgent need to recover that sense of a developing American character Crane's account has taken leave of. Whether commentators attack this lack of character directly as General McClurg does in denouncing Private Fleming as a coward, or denounce it after a manner subtle enough to remain unconscious of it, as do more recent critics, by reading a coherent line of character development into the arbitrary incidents in Henry's life, the wish remains the same in both cases, to recover the sense of exemplary continuity, integrity, and significance for those Civil War events Stephen Crane has forcibly excised from official history. Crane acknowledges the urgency of this need by never failing to drive a wedge between the sheer contingency of Henry's battle experiences and those reflections on them that never account for so much as they displace these incidents with other concerns. What results is an ongoing sense of disorientation, a knowledge of Henry Fleming's involvement in a battle that history will later turn into a monumental event, but whose dimensions never presently convert into anything more than a series of discontinuous incidents, followed by pauses whose emptiness Henry can never fill with sufficient reflections. Without adequate ideological underpinnings these battle scenes flare up as severe emotional and psychic blows without the

consolation recognition brings. Instead of absorbing Henry's recollections and the experiences they are meant to describe into the continuities
of a narrative, *The Red Badge of Courage* underwrites the absence of continuity in a war that never achieves the epic qualities either Henry or
a nation of historians would impose on it.

Indeed the war Henry suffers through seems, in its tendency seemingly to start from the beginning with each encounter, to lack any
historical attributes whatever. Unlike the America that found its past
confirmed and its geography decisively marked by war, Henry Fleming can discover no frame capable of situating him securely in either
time or place. With each explosive battlefield encounter, Henry discovers
that the barrier against too much stimulation has been breached, that
the recognitions following these encounters and the anticipations meant
to prepare him for them are both painfully inadequate. Confronted
repeatedly with shocks utterly disrespectful of that lag between recollec-
tion and healing forgetfulness when experience has the time to form,
Henry witnesses scenes that even when able to leave marks in the
memory do so by quite literally leaving him out. In the following scene,
for example, Henry records, with a lucidity heightened through his
fears, a series of impressions released from the control of any fixed
reference point:

> It seemed to the youth that he saw everything. Each blade
> of green grass was bold and clear. He thought that he was
> aware of each change in the thin, transparent vapor that
> floated idly in sheets. The brown or grey trunks showed each
> roughness of their surfaces. And the men of the regiment,
> with their staring eyes and sweating faces running madly,
> or falling as if thrown headlong, to queer, heaped-up
> corpses—all were comprehended. His mind took a
> mechanical but firm impression, so that afterward everything
> was pictured and explained to him save why he himself was
> there.

In this description, each colorful image surges up as all foreground,
with a suddenness whose intensity is unmediated by a context capable
of either subduing or containing it. Instead of settling into that relationship in which a figure is clearly contextualized within a stable
ground and which a coherent picture is supposed to guarantee, these
"firm impressions" glare out as if in defiance of an implicit order to
move into perspective. Not only the individual impressions fail to

modify one another, however; so do the sentences in which they appear. These sentences do not describe a sequence in which new facts are "comprehended" by an overall principle of coherence. Without any perspective capable of sorting out the relevant from the irrelevant, everything crowds into Henry's consciousness with all the force of confusion. Thus the very givenness of this jumble of impressions renders redundant Henry's concluding observation that everything was explained to him save his own presence in the scene.

In this scene, then, the exclusion of any coherent perspective begins to function as a perspective, one sufficiently powerful to make audible Henry's unspoken reaction, his sensed alienation from the scene he observes. In this account, however, Henry Fleming does not assert his alienation as a feeling of separation. If anything he seems utterly absorbed in the picture he describes. He seems so utterly consumed in a battle scene in the act of manifesting itself as to be indistinguishable from what he perceives. Because, however, what he perceives are little more than sheer impressions, unrelieved by any signification whatsoever, it would be more accurate to say that what Fleming perceives is not a conventional battle scene but the loss of any framework capable of informing this scene with significance. In this scene then he becomes absorbed not in a picture but its loss, the disappearance of what grounds a picture in a significant frame of reference.

By representing such "private" impressions unverified by either the accounts of other veterans or historians of the war, Crane depicts a character incompatible enough with the nation's self-portrait to elicit General McClurg's fear of "foreign" influence. For Henry's chance observations, in the radical incongruity of their sheer givenness, do indeed permit the past to speak in an unfamiliar voice. This voice, in the very strangeness of its inflection, unsettles both the nation's past and the character sanctioned by it. Moreover, when carefully listened to, this voice fabricates a "reality" able to invest the past with an uncanny sense of immediacy, but an immediacy interlaced with an irony unlimited enough to relegate this past to a realm of irretrievable pastness.

It would be a mistake, however, to suggest that this voice dominates the narrative line of the *The Red Badge of Courge;* it cannot be accommodated by narrative conventions. Narration, in converting the mere succession of incidents into a meaningful sequence, silences the voice released in the chance encounter. Like a photograph of a battle scene with the captions cut off, this voice counts any explanation capable of guaranteeing a coherent context or selecting out the significant details among the casualities of war. It speaks *through* the impressions surviving Henry's presence at scenes of battles, and by speaking through these incidental details asserts their independence from the war story Henry has to tell. Indeed this voice sustains itself by converting Henry's statements about the war back into pieces of it, so that what gets narrated in *The Red Badge of Courage* never coincides with those incidents that can never be explained but only marked.

If in scenes like the one cited, Henry's impressions denote his awareness of everything except a rationale for his being there, his narration forcibly displaces these impressions by supplying a missing rationale. Thus, the narrative inscribes a discrepancy between the self-image Henry wishes to represent and the incidents that fail to engage any image of the self whatsoever. Given that these marked incidents occupy a different space from those narrated events Henry creates through an act of reflection, the reader must engage this work with a double vision. Once envisioned through this double perspective, however, *The Red Badge of Courage* reveals a conception of the self that is perhaps as much a victim of narrative conventions as the vicissitudes of war. Having begun this discussion with a reflection on the incompatibility between Henry's chance incidents and conventional representations of the Civil War, we are drawn by the very force of this discrepancy to another interpretation, one guided by Henry's struggles to confer a significance on events that would otherwise utterly confound him. Through such an interpretive strategy we feel the pressure first of the merely chance encounter and then the force of Henry's need to recall those incidents in the mold of a meaningful narrative. In many cases the irrational force of the war proves a sufficient rationale to justify Henry's need for a significant narration. But Crane's text is remarkable for its refusal to favor the meaningful narrative. By persistently locating Henry in the space between unrelieved contingency and imposed narrative, Crane inveigles the arbitrariness usually associated with the chance event into the orderly narrative sequence. More startlingly, however, through this organization of materials, Crane exposes the need to choose Henry's narrative instead of his experience as still another narrative convention.

Perhaps we cannot acknowledge the force of this recognition until we ascertain the daring implication of Crane's narrative strategies. In the arrangement of his plot, Crane did not use the brutality of the war as a pretext for justifying the humane values implicit in narrative conventions. Crane's chronology inverts the one we have described.

In *The Red Badge of Courage,* narratives do not follow battles and provide needed explanation; instead they precede and indeed demand
battles as elaborations and justifications of already narrated events.

"Private" Fleming negotiates this "turn of events" in that moment of reflection he secures for himself in the wake of the excitement
following Jim Conklin's "rumor" that the troops are about to move.
In the course of his reflection Henry does not, as do so many of his
fictional and nonfictional predecessors, envision himself in a project
involving the liberation of slaves. The only mention of a Negro in the
entire novel appears in the fourth paragraph, when Jim Conklin's tale
creates a state of confusion that quite literally abandons the Negro's
cause. "When he had finished, the blue-clothed men scattered into small
arguing groups between the rows of squat brown huts. A negro teamster
who had been dancing upon a cracker box with the hilarious encouragement of twoscore soldiers was deserted. He sat mournfully down."
Without any "noble" causes to commandeer his martial emotions,
Henry's musings fill this vacuum by turning to "tales of great movement" as opportunities for personal aggrandizement. These battles,
Henry reflected, "might not be distinctly Homeric, but there seemed
to be much glory in them." Having already read of marches, sieges,
conflicts, Henry now "longed to see it all." His busy mind had drawn
for him large pictures "extravagant in color, lurid with breathless deeds";
it remained for him to "realize" these narrated pictures with matching
deeds. In the reflections that inevitably follow all of his battle experiences, then, it is obvious that Henry tries to take possession of
himself as the figure he had previously imagined occupying center stage
in one of these extravagant pictures. What may not be obvious, however,
is that Henry's means of taking possession of himself share nothing
with his battlefield ordeals. Battle narratives and conventions from these
narratives provide Henry both with the practice and the position of
his acts of self-reflection. Moreover, these conventions replace the battle
condition Henry survives with previously narrated battle scenes. And
these representations impinge on lived scenes with sufficient pressure
for Henry to measure the adequacy of his response against these
representations.

At this juncture, however, Henry's narrative qualifies rather significantly an earlier observation. For in disclosing the distinction between his "narrated self" and actual experiences, Henry does not elide
but reveals the rift between the incidents beyond telling and the telltale
narrative that displaces them. Even more remarkable, however, is

what else Henry implies in his innocent disclosure of his motives for going to war. For if Henry enlisted to appropriate, upon reflection, images of his own aggrandizement, he did not really wish to see action in battle at all. Action in battle was only an alibi for his need to fulfill a preoccupation, gleaned through diligent reading of war narratives, with action at a distance, his ability to take possession of the world through images of an overwhelming effect upon it. As Henry himself indicates in his reflections following the first battle, war exists as a testing ground to prove the power to turn the world into signs of the individual's advance upon it:

> So it was all over at last! The supreme trial has been passed. The red, formidable difficulties of war had been vanquished. He went into an ecstasy of self-satisfaction. He had the most delightful sensations of his life. Standing as if apart from himself, he viewed that last scene. He perceived that the man who had fought thus was magnificent. He felt that he was a fine fellow. He saw himself with even those ideals which he had considered as far beyond him.

While it will take a later scene for Henry to acknowledge the distinction between the "image" of "himself" gained after the fact through reflection, and the shocking battle incidents exceeding in their overwhelming immediacy the self's ability either to have experiences or to reflect upon them, it takes no longer than the eve of his first encounter for Henry to delineate the frightening dimensions of the terrible logic at work in war. "From his home his youthful eyes had looked upon war in his own country with distrust. It must be some sort of play affair." The double bind at work in these two starkly phrased sentences lashes out with all the force of a compulsion. Henry must go to war to realize the glories previously only narrated, but once at war he inevitably discovers the need for a narrative to displace actual wartime incidents incompatible with a reality legitimized by and *as* narration. In other words, the "play" war that Henry would "realize" by going into battle upholds no necessary similarity with actual battle conditions; only the conventions of a narration that Henry, through reflection, can read into these insufferable conditions can confer the appearance of "reality" upon these otherwise aberrant circumstances. This is to say that Henry's reflections constitute efforts to reread narratives he had taken to heart prior to taking up the Union colors. When considered in this perspective, however, war does not seem an arbitrary congeries of contingent circumstances. Instead it imparts a sense of the necessary limit to, and indeed the reprieve from, the excesses of already narrated "reality." Crane exploits the contradictions implicit in this perspective when he suggests that Henry's motive for going to war may be nothing more than his wish to coincide with the extravagant deeds, the "*broken*-bladed" exploits attributed to the heroes of traditional war narratives. Consequently not even the "private" wishes are even truly "his" own but migrate to him from a "generalized" subject of conventional war stories Henry, with all the secret shame of a raw recruit, tries to feel equal to. In *The Red Badge of Courage,* then, Henry Fleming must feel alienated in turn both by those incidents that portend their inaccessibility to significance but also by the very narratives intended to impose significance upon them. Thus from a vantage point quite different from Henry's we begin to understand the urgency of his need to take possession of the war in personal terms. Involved in incidents unable to be retrieved in human terms, Henry must invent a history for himself that would at least guarantee the continuity of his identity, and at best alleviate the pressure of those incidents he merely lives through. In other words, Henry's narrative does not exist as his means of recording events of war as his principal strategy for taking possession of "his" life.

REPRESENTATIONS AND FEAR

Ironically, however, the only way he can truly possess "his" life in a narrative leads him to assert the independence of his narrative, from those literally surrounding him. To prevent "his" absorption in "their" narratives, Henry, on the eve of the first battle, develops a rather perverse tactic. First he acknowledges his debt to already written war narratives by recalling the inspiration he drew from accounts of those soldiers whose extravagant deeds relieved the boredom of his days at home, but then in a curious turn he dramatizes the return to "his" senses by indulging in doubts over his ability to replicate their feats. Surprisingly, these doubts do not lessen Henry's feelings of self-regard but heighten them. Indeed Henry's musings draw a compelling line of connection between fantasies of personal failure and newly discovered personal resources sufficiently different from the conventional to authorize a "private" identity. Positioned between events that alienate him through excessive shock and already narrated events that replace his exploits with those of traditional heroes, Henry charges this space between impossible alternatives by fearing "his" cowardice. Through this fear, Henry makes a virtue of his dispossession by converting this depersonalized separation from both narrated and actual events into a personal act of choice. Without any abstract moral principle to organize and legitimize his behavior, he feels compelled to develop an ethos of fear as his basis for unique personality. His fear asserts its distinct quality by supplanting the threat to personal integrity usually associated with an object of fear. Instead of a threat Henry discovers hidden reserves strong enough to withstand prospects that would otherwise prove utterly self-destructive.

Consequent to a series of reflections inspired by his fear, Henry feels free to conceive of himself as a figure set apart from the representations of his comrades. A "mental outcast," he must abandon all preconceptions, his own as well as those in the narratives he had earlier consumed so avidly, for "in this crisis the previously learned laws of life proved useless." Instead of a feeling of disgrace, a sense of self-discovery and a challenge to his habitual modes of understanding result from his unparalleled fear. "Whatever he had learned of himself was of no avail. He was an unknown quality. He saw that he would again be obliged to experiment as he had in his earlier youth." Confronted, in other words, with emotions that made him "feel strange in the presence" of the other men, Henry made the most of his estrangement. Refusing to conceive of himself as a fixed object of "their" derision, Henry explores the range of "his" feelings on the subject of his fear, until in the course of these reflections he decides that fear not only sets him apart from the other men but it also situates him above them. On the eve of his first battle experience, Henry invests fear with enough privilege to suggest that "he must break from the ranks and harangue his comrades. . . . The generals were idiots to send them marching into a regular pen. There was but one pair of eyes in the corps." Fear, in other words, enables Henry to enact a drama of his powerlessness reassuring enough in its ancillary benefits to convert his "private" sector into a position of sufficient exemplary power to make his reflections superior to those of the generals. This drama reaches its peak when Henry, in an ecstasy of rejection, imagines the other men reacting derisively not to his fear but to the "refined perceptions" resulting from it. And the advance in rank secured by this imagined humiliation enables Henry to situate himself outside the context of all previously written war narratives, as he assumes "the demeanor of one who knows that he is doomed alone to unwritten responsibilities."

Through fear, Henry discovers the power to shape what he takes to be the "original" style of his powerlessness. Consequently, when he actually takes his part in a battle and does not run away in fear, he experiences this failure to run away not as an influx of courage, the reversal familiar from conventional war narratives, but as a loss of those privileges in rank that fear conferred upon him. So instead of continuing to conceive of himself as set apart from the ranks, in battle Henry "suddenly lost concern for himself . . . became not a man but a member." Surrounded by the din and roar of combat, Henry, working his rifle "like an automatic affair," cannot take the time to know fear. Rather, he feels a "brotherhood" with his comrades, yet a brotherhood that does not result from a shared sense of purpose. Deprived of a humane cause to motivate them, the members of this "brotherhood" lose all signs of human purposiveness and seem less like a group of men and more like a "firework that, ignited, proceeds superior to circumstances until its blazing vitality fades." Because preparation for this first battle is secured through the consciousness of a private who had already made much of his dispossession, what comes as the greater shock is not Fleming's reduction in stature to the level of a "beast" or an automaton but his loss of those "private" daydreams that formerly enabled him to take possession of that alienation. During this incident, Fleming could not continue to brood over his fear but "lost concern for himself" and fell into a battle sleep emptied of his dreams and witnessed all "as one who dozes."

We have already considered Fleming's first reaction to his initiation into battle. He uses it as an opportunity to appropriate from a distance representations of his ability to measure up to the "red formidable difficulties of war." As if to underscore the falsity of these representations, however, Fleming combines them with "ideals which he considered far beyond him" and which had no influence on his decision to enlist. Following his first battle, then, Private Fleming fears his apparently courageous battle actions misrepresent him. When his reflections on the battle turn up a Henry Fleming who did not feel fear, Henry is jubilant at the discovery of an ideal representation of himself, but his joy diminishes when he considers that this ideal is sufficiently at odds with the self-image he has been manufacturing to constitute a loss of himself.

SHAME

Moreover, when he finally does run away, during the second

encounter, he finds fear a sufficiently generalized response to cease to be "his" private reaction. We do not realize the significance Henry derives from this loss, however, until the very end of his narrative, when, upon reflecting on his victorious encounter, Henry once again feels gratified over his apparently heroic behavior. This time, however, after he spends "delightful minutes viewing the gilded images of memory," his thoughts return to his action on the first day, whereupon he fails to recall his initial encounter altogether. Instead of recollecting the scene in which he actually outlasted the enemy assault, he can remember only his desertion in the field, chronologically the second incident, as having happened first: "The ghost of his flight from the first engagement appeared to him and danced. . . . For a moment he blushed and the light of his soul flickered with shame." This lapse of memory is understandable enough when we recall the trancelike state he continuously falls into when battles actually begin. Another context for understanding this lapse emerges, however, when we recall how effective fear was in enabling Henry to take possession of his alienation. During that first battle Henry effectively forgot his fear, so following the logic sanctioned by his psychic economy, we can infer that this fear, which underwrote Private Fleming's inscription within a coherent narrative, upon returning to consciousness erased Henry's memory of the "first engagement." Yet given Henry's former correlation of his identity with his prolonged dream of fear, this memory lapse was almost an inevitability. Indeed this lapse seems less attributable to Henry's memory than to the loss in this instance of any identity. Without fear, Henry lacks the state of mind capable of conferring the privileges of a continuous identity upon him. Moreover, as a reproduction of those heroic representations familiar from all the narratives he had previously read, Henry's reflections on that first engagement were not "his" any more than they were those of any other member of his regiment. They were postures and actions that belonged to no one precisely because they were the "commonplaces" of war stories. After he finally does run away in fear, Henry does not return to battle intent on recovering the attitude he displaced during that first battle, but to recover that great dream of fear he lost when he fell into battle sleep.

In Henry's eyes, the greatest casuality of war was the loss of those psychic resources he needed to mobilize in order to countermand the anticipated derision and consequent shame he would inevitably experience when others found out about his fear. In the moment that he runs, Henry, like the men he saw retreating from the field before his first battle experience, is not even conscious of the presence of an audience. Like the "proverbial chicken," Henry, cut off from any rationale for his actions, could only save face after the fact by reactivating his earlier daydreams of cowardice and shame. Without an abstract moral principle capable of absorbing his actions into reality, Henry is condemned to "realize" his daydreams. Involved as he is in actions irrelevant to the mastery of any human subject, Henry can only redefine himself as a human subject by willfully conceiving of himself as an object of derision. In short, Henry Fleming who was formerly subject to the delusions of fear, after the second battle engagement releases all the resources of what we might call the subject of fear.

While he runs, Henry replaces his blind fear with fear rationalized, and from this transformed position he recognizes his former deeds. For example, when he runs away from the scene of battle, Henry runs into a scene that reenacts almost precisely the conditions of his first battle engagement. In this quite literal version of a recognition scene, Henry, upon seeing the regiment hold its ground, does not interpret this behavior as a sign of valor but pities the men for being "methodical idiots, machine-like fools." With this recognition, however, Henry does not merely replace the earlier role of hero with the role of deserter, though his ability to play both roles with equal reason does expose the interchangeability of the roles of hero and deserter. In judging as mechanical an earlier version of his activity that might otherwise be interpreted as courageous, he displays the privileges released by desertion. Instead of feeling judged by the men in the field he finds them to be merely elements engaged in strategic maneuvers. By co-opting their accusation, he thereby defuses in advance any judgment these men might level against him. Ironically enough, it is only when Henry is in a position of defensive reaction that he feels in sufficient command of himself to speak with authority.

At this point in the narrative, however, an even deeper irony intervenes. For the only discourse that Henry feels sufficiently powerful as a defense of his desertion is a discourse that has already been spoken. Unable to defend his desertion alone, he must enlist the support of a Nature who "would die if its timid eyes were compelled to see blood." On the eve of the first battle scene, Henry prepared himself for the inadequacy of this attribution of a maternal role to nature. Prior to going to battle he had primed himself for a beautiful scene of departure, one wherein his mother, like the mothers of the Greek epics, was to respond with great pathos to the tragic news of his departure, but not even his mother proved sufficiently maternal to fulfill his superstitions; "she had disappointed him by saying nothing whatever about returning with his shield or on it." We need only recall Henry's earlier "flash of astonishment," the irreconcilability between the apparent indifference of Nature to War and the concern Nature should be demonstrating, to see the wishful thinking in this conception. After all the noise and din of that first battle, Henry looked up at the blue sky and realized that "Nature had gone tranquilly on with her golden process in the midst of so much devilment." Whenever Fleming looks to Nature for signs of grief or solace, Nature responds not with a look of indifference but with the demeanor of one who has already completed the work of mourning for a lost beloved. Instead of functioning as a support system, Nature, like Henry's mother, seems to have subscribed to a series of representations enabling it to explain Henry's death as a commonplace occurrence. If anything, this scene only visually reenacts what Henry's mother had said much earlier:" 'If so be a time comes when you have to be kilt . . . why, Henry, don't think of anything 'cept what's right, because there's many a woman has to bear up 'ginst sech things these times, and the Lord'll take care of us all.' "

In such scenes as these, Crane takes pains to separate Henry's wish to envision Nature as "a woman with a deep aversion to tragedy" from the enlistment of Nature to underwrite and hence "naturalize" such totally contradictory sentiments as those expressed by Henry's mother. Henry dramatizes this need to use Nature as a mode of legitimizing action when, upon seeing a squirrel "run chattering with fear" from a pine cone thrown by him, he interprets this behavior as Nature's sign corroborating his desertion. Then, inspired by this unlooked for support, he intensifies the authority of this sign until it reads like a mandate. "There was a law, he said. . . . The squirrel, immediately upon recognizing danger, had taken to his legs without ado." In the very next paragraph, however, Henry records a sign that fails to reenforce his argument but seemingly reenacts his feeling of being helplessly trapped. So when he sees "out at some black water, a small animal pounce in and emerge directly with a gleaming fish," Henry cannot assimilate this action to his theme of Nature's sympathy for his plight. Like the battle incidents before it, then, this scene flashes into consciousness as an impression closed to reflection, not so much an empty perception as a perception inimical to the categories of representation enlisted to convert perception into cognition.

Henry's desertion is of course no more sanctioned by the "nature" of things than is the war he flees, but the need to seek this sanction is the same in both cases. And the moment Henry uses Nature to justify his desertion marks a turning point in the narrative. In the incidents prior to his flight, Henry converts his fear into *unrealized* fantasies of desertion and thereby recovers an identity by making the most of *his* dispossession. But the moment he wishes to justify his actual desertion he must use the favorite strategy of the forces mobilized against him: the enlistment of Nature as a principal agent in a narrative designed to justify a course of action. In choosing a narrative to justify his actions, however, Henry abandons his charged position between battle incidents and already related events. For instead of continuing to resist them, he chooses to appropriate preexistent narratives as signs of the validity of his choice. Henry's choice of Nature, rather than Slavery or Union or martial heroism, as the final arbiter for his action proves more telling than any use to which he might put Nature. By definition the most fundamental because the least derivative of the narrative discourses at Henry's disposal, Nature and representation sanctioned by the discourse of Nature promise to be the most reliable arbiters of action and perception. So when Henry entertains a "natural" perception, like that of the trapped fish, irrelevant to the discourse of Nature he has been pursuing, he must either register that perception but take no notice of it or force it to cohere with the narrative he has been elaborating. In view of his efforts to include all of Nature within a uniform framework of representation, however, a perception uninformed with the privileges of that representation must have impinged on Henry's consciousness like a wound, a mark of what has been cut away from an organized whole.

RAGE

In *The Red Badge of Courage,* Crane focuses less on Henry's attempts to recover coherence by imposing an interpretation than on his failures. For, as we have seen, in these failures Henry repeatedly recovers the force of his character as its inaccessibility to preexistent forms. Whereas Henry formerly elaborated this inaccessibility into compelling dreams supervised by fear, in the course of the desertion that realizes "his" dream, Henry confronts a visionary figure terrifying enough to make even his dream of fear seem ghostly by comparison. Possessed by the need to justify his desertion, Henry happens upon the figure of a dying soldier who should have provided just the occasion Henry needs to give desertion a persuasive rationale. Turned into a ghost of himself by the battle incidents that converted him into just another casualty of war and the war narrative that sacrificed his life to its purposes, this "spectral soldier" effectively marks the point of intersection of the two great forces of alienation Henry equally fears. As the horrible double effect of both battle and battle narratives, Conklin's death should have the power to provide Henry's fear with the justification even Nature failed to supply. When confronted, however, with this horrible justification, Henry does not find still another corroboration for his desertion but a limit to all attempts to justify any activity whatever. Faced with the figure swelled with the redoubled force of alienation, Henry discovers the inadequacy of every attempt at justification. When we recall that it was Conklin, waving his arms in enthusiastic sympathy with the exciting news of troop movement, who awoke Henry's earlier fears, we get a sense of the full extent of their loss. Moreover, when we perceive the spastic arm movements released by his death as after-images of the arm-waving enthusiasm that earlier accompanied Jim's tales of war, we get an uncanny sense of witnessing in this literal correlation of narration and existence not simply the destruction of Jim Conklin but the loss of the power of narration to inform existence. In this scene, Henry mourns both the loss of his friend and the loss of a narration intended to represent this loss. Upon recognizing the identity of the "spectral soldier," Henry comprehends through this terrible recognition the shadowy limitations of his great dream of fear. Conklin's death interrupts Henry's attempt to rationalize his fear at the very moment Henry needs it most urgently, or rather it permanently separates the shock enveloped within his fear from any recognition capable of relieving it. Conklin's death, as the intersection of alienating forces released by battles and narratives, thereby supplants Henry's cowardice in that charged place between actual and narrated events. Henry recovers this space, however, when he turns his urgent need to supply the rationale for his fear into rage over the absence of any rationale whatsoever. This rage expresses itself not through the constraints of discursive narratives but through the breakdown of any attempt to constrain it into meaning:

> The youth turned with sudden, livid rage toward the battlefield. He shook his fist. He seemed about to deliver a philippic.
> "Hell— "

The red sun was pasted in the sky like a [fierce] wafer.

Instead of being discharged into a "philippic," a convention that socializes rage into a manageable expression of loss, Henry's rage breaks down into a threatening impression, one that glares back at him with all the fury of its inaccessibility to his context. In registering this impression at this moment, Crane does not secretly subscribe to the doctrine of naturalism. As a cultural movement, naturalism only justified man's advance upon nature by reflecting back the force of his encroachment as if it were the course of Nature. Nor does this impression "symbolize" Henry's reaction. Like the color that dominates it, this impression renders visible only a glaring surface. Henry's registration of this perception in place of the philippic marks a transformation in his mode of accommodating himself to events. Formerly, Henry actively ignored events and scenes his representation could not appropriate. After emptying Henry's perception of such vast ideological issues as the liberation of the slaves and the recovery of the Union, Crane investigates perception reduced, as it were, to its least common denominators. In the absence of abstract moral and political principles, fear and shame restore coherence and significance to perception even as they circumscribe its locus. Disrespectful of the seeming irrelevance of Private Fleming's apperception to the events surrounding him, fear and shame intervene and replace Fleming's sense of the sheer contingency of what actually transpires with a conventional drama, proceeding from fear and into desertion but holding out the promise of a triumphant recovery of courage.

By holding out the promise of a recovered mastery, the discourse of fear installs Henry in a position to record and reflect upon his perceptions; thus he can later narrate his adventures. Neither the discourse of fear nor that of shame proves innocent of ideological consideration. By underwriting every other representation they constitute the least common denominators, the constraints of ideological representation. Unlike either fear or shame, rage acts out the loss of what can never be possessed. Utterly inimical to the claims for coherence and privileged responsibility formerly secured through shame and fear, rage replaces their reflective appropriation of perceptions and actions after the fact with the loss of any fact whatsoever to reflect upon. When enraged, Henry no longer fears being gazed at by another any more than he feels ashamed before the judgment of his projected ego ideals. Instead he becomes so completely absorbed in the loss of any representation capable of doing justice to what he perceives that all of the energy of perception seems to have been redirected. In such scenes as that of the interrupted philippic, Henry does not speak from the position of one who reflects upon a scene. Unable to be begin a philippic on the injustices of war, Henry instead notices that "the red sun was pasted in the sky like a [fierce] wafer." And he seems so utterly identified in this remark with what would otherwise sanction a thoughtful outburst of despair and frustration as to fail his official duties as a subject. Instead of looking at the red sun, he seems to be looking out from its red surface with all the intensity of a glaring rebuke. Consequently the sentence does not express so much as it restores the rage generating it, nets the loss of what grounds it. Through this impression, Henry acknowledges both the undischargeable force of an event that cannot be assimilated to the Nature of things, and all in Nature that cannot be accommodated to man's need to impose an interpretation. And he accompanies this dual recognition with all the fury of an unmet demand.

In this scene, rage displaces fear and shame as Henry's response to his failure to be assimilated by either actual or narrated events. Through rage, however, Henry does not rest content with a recovery of his sense of dispossession as was the case with the prolonged dream of fear. Rage turns Henry's feelings of impotence into an overwhelming power, for when he is enraged his sense of total loss makes absolute demands on the world. Rage, as the power released through a reaction to power's loss, effectively separates the power of alienation from its cause. When Henry discovers the power released by rage, it is impossible to distinguish the power Henry fights with from the power Henry fights against. This is not to say as was the case with his fear that Henry identifies with either preexistent narrations or battle conditions as his means of justifying his rage. Rage disrupts the line of demarcation between agent and action, system and circumstance, throwing everything into a state of confusion.

When I suggest that Henry replaces cowardice with rage in that charged space between equally alienating alternatives, I do not mean that Henry never fears cowardice again. Earlier Henry's fear that he would fail to measure up released a compensatory belief in the superiority of his perspective. He needed to believe his fear was privileged because "he" felt anonymous, a veritable unknown soldier in the midst of vast actions performed by vast collections of men. Through fear he converts his suspicion that "he" will never be recognized into a discovery of a previously unknown element in his psyche, a cowardice that distinguishes him by setting him apart from his fellows. In the course of events, Henry makes the desertion implicit in this feeling of being apart explicit when he actually runs from the field. When he seeks to render his desertion privileged by articulating its unique rationale, he identifies with all the conventional narratives that justify war by aligning it with the nature of things he earlier found so oppressive. After his confrontation with Jim Conklin, however, he not only recognizes the limitations of this rationale but also fears this limit. In other words, the fear of cowardice that led him to flee the field has become differently valenced. Without any effective rationale to recover the superiority in his former position of "mental outcast," Henry can only identify with a rage that acknowledges total loss and transforms loss into power.

Having experienced the absolute loss of all his former claims, Henry reactivates his fear of being judged a coward not in order to secure the sense of his superior rationale but in order to react with rage against the inadequacy of all rationales. His fear of being judged a coward, in other words, once the sole motivating force for his actions, becomes a pretext for his rage against any viable motivation whatsoever.

After the Conklin incident, Henry no longer feels shame. Shame after all presupposes a prior feeling of belonging to a community capable of making one feel alienated by shame. In his discovery of the limits of his rationale, Henry also discovers the limits of the community justified by it. Through various narrative devices, Crane suggests that the basis for this socializing process is not a shared purpose but a common fear of becoming a figure of public shame. As has been suggested, the ideological power of this process derives from Henry's belief that fear confers a "private" identity upon him. But throughout the narrative, Crane signals the "general" state of this fear by interrupting his "private" fantasy of cowardice with its implicit expressions by others. When every soldier seems engaged in the same "private struggle," this struggle cannot be "his" but must be "theirs" or no one's. After Henry's long reverie of shameful fear prior to that first incident, to offer only the most salient example, the "loud soldier" Wilson indicates his participation in the same "privileged" drama of fear as Henry's when he blurts out a plea that Henry send home, after Wilson's death in the field, packets of letters to his mother. Crane suggests that the very feelings of fear and cowardice capable of releasing the illusion of "privacy" have already been overcoded and directed toward common military aims. And Crane signals this abuse by turning what should be a "private" first-person form into a third-person narrative. For through this narrative strategy Henry's most private thoughts turn out not to be his but "theirs" after all.

After his encounter with Conklin, Henry attempts to regain his shame, but now he knows only "the ghost of shame," the rage he has not been socialized out of. Following the Conklin incident, Henry needs to feel the shame he earlier feared. Shame, after all, would make him feel the inadequacy of some judgment. But Henry always finds the position of shame preoccupied by his rage over its inadequacy. That is why he reacts with such violence when the tattered soldier asks him where he is wounded. A wound would be a justification for leaving the field, and Henry, in discovering the inadequacy of all attempts at justification, has carried his desertion too far. So when he runs back to the field he does not wish to prove himself to the other soldiers— that would only corroborate the adequacy of their categories—but to represent to them the "magnificent pathos" of his rage by dying right in front of them. In short, he wishes to bring "their" judgment up against "his" rage.

Paradoxically, however, Henry's means of reentering the military world is not through a demarcation of his rage but through an apparent identification with that world's ability to judge. A head wound, received when he grabs a deserter and asks for an explanation of his desertion, facilitates this turn of events. The head wound, in its openness to ambiguous interpretation, is what the deserter gives Henry instead of what he asked for, an explanation for desertion. This wound, like the sheer contingency of the battle scenes, is utterly unassimilable to the moral discourse of courage or cowardice. As the record of what gets perceived once privileged representations lose their power to master an event, this wound marks on Henry's body the equivalent to the locus of those losses "the red sun pasted in the sky like a wafer" burned into his consciousness. However much the other men might try to impress this wound to the scale of judgment adjudicated by either courage or cowardice, this wound fails to represent anything but the breakdown of the procedures of judgment. As the mark on his body not of any particular moral code but of his having been *cut off* from those codes, Henry's wound turns every attempt to interpret it as a sign of courage into a vast charade of judgment. Through an identification with this wound, Henry can return to his regiment not as a "member" reincorporated into the "body" of men, but as a wound, a mark of what has already been cut off from the body.

This is not to say that upon returning Henry refuses to engage in judicial exchanges, but that the resultant charade of justice differs significantly from Henry's earlier experience. When in order to forestall Wilson's harsh rebuke of him for fleeing the field, Henry calls Wilson a coward and points to that packet of letters as proof, he performs that same activity of co-optation of judgment enacted earlier in the day. When he delivers this judgment, however, a judgment he himself fears, he does not judge Wilson so much as he converts the feeling of being judged wrongly into a judgment—a judgment whose inadequacy he knows from within the position of the judge. Thus Henry's secret revenge against it disrupts the very judicial system he seems in the service of. To socialize this behavior Henry reactivates that same narrative of the gifted man protected by Nature he used earlier to rationalize his desertion. But neither discourse brings his rage to justice. Each instead leaves a residue, a reaction against his distortions, and recovers for Henry the anger he can only discharge through the fury of his actions in battle.

Upon his return, as a more profound outcast, a figure all the more tellingly "cut off" from his peers than the man who deserted, Henry does not recover his place but reactivates his rage against all that displaces him. Nor does he actually fear the judgments of others, but demands these judgments as excuses for vengeance. When a general curses Henry's regiment for a pack of mule drivers, Henry is grateful for the chance to localize his rage on the general. When he fights on the field he does not fight Confederate soldiers but wages war on the discourses that formerly placed him so securely as a private in the military: he wounds his fear of cowardice with a fury in excess of any judgment and destroys his fear of shame with actions outrageous enough to make all the other soldiers feel ashamed by contrast. Henry, who earlier felt cursed and ashamed by his inability to live up to the heroics demanded by war, displays such extravagant brutality on the field that he becomes a general's means of cursing and shaming other men into battle. But Henry is no longer inspired by heroic representations. His apparent courage derives from the sense that he has already been marked as a casualty of war. Having formerly identified himself with all the representations gleaned from his battle narratives, once he loses those representations Henry fights with all the reckless abandon of one who has already been lost in battle.

Neither cowardly nor courageous, in his elemental fury and rage he arouses the need of those around him to reduce him to this code. Henry has already despaired of a world that the dialectic of courage and cowardice would idealize him back into. In battle he does not discover a personal identity resistant to the mutual dispossession of both actual and narrated events, but revenges himself against the delusions of a private identity and replaces identity with the force of its abandonment. His rage preoccupies every position, whether on the battlefield, in society, or in the narrations that "realize" them all, with a vengeance over the inevitability of their loss. By the end of the novel, then, rage has ceased to be a mere theme and has replaced shame and fear, the principal agents of ideological construction, with the power of its destruction.

When in rage, Henry performs actions that cannot be assimilated by any narrative: they emerge with all the accidental force of battle incidents. Rage replaces duration with immediacy, reflection with "glare," appropriation after the fact with loss as what takes the place of fact. After his final battle scene, when Henry accepts the description of his behavior as courageous, his frame of acceptance does not silence his rage, nor does his memory of the moment of desertion repress his fury. In this moment of acceptance, when fear and shame return with all the force of repressed representation, however, Henry does reveal the opposition between courage and rage, and the narrative that implements it, to be the official means of being absorbed back into the world.

Some of Henry's rage reappears, however, when we recall what Henry does not: that Henry earlier felt alienated by this traditional narrative into which he now willingly reinscribes himself. By way of conclusion, we could begin a list of the many shocks of representation, its inadequacy to the situations it should inform with meaning. We could begin this list, moreover, with shock at our recognition of the completely different social worlds separating the dialect Henry Fleming uses when he actually speaks in the novel from the refined discourse of moral discrimination representing his frame of mind throughout. Whenever we begin such a list, however, we cannot fail to include Henry's decision at the end of the novel apparently to continue to rehearse the discourse that unfailingly misrepresents him throughout. If almost a century of critics have cushioned this shock by subscribing to the conventions of "character development," "fear overcome," "recovered responsibility," and "mature judgment," authorized by Henry's final narrative, we begin to recover some of its force when we recall General McClurg's fierce denunciation. Unlike most commentators, the general does not feel persuaded by Henry's final narrative. Instead of commending him for returning to his duty, the general needs to call Henry a coward, a Northerner who fled from the field, and a British sympathizer. The overreaction implicit in the general's ideological overcoding indicates that he, like Henry Fleming, feels the inadequacy of these terms to account for the experiences of war. Thus, however thoroughly he may repudiate Henry's actions, he finally feels persuaded enough by Henry's rage to use his denunciation of Henry's actions as his means of sharing that rage. Indeed his rage does not emanate from disagreement over Henry's actions in battle but from the failure of his own ideology to do justice to experiences in battle. Moreover, when we reread Henry's decision to use guilt and shame as his own private debriefing ceremony from the general's perspective, another implication of Henry's choice comes into view. Henry always deployed guilt and shame as his means of making moral claims on events utterly beyond the control of any individual. At the end of the novel, however, the guilt Henry feels cannot be ascribed to his failure to measure up to a battle narrative. The source of his shame, the tattered soldier, is not a representative of moral responsibility. Neither a coward nor a hero, the tattered soldier remains etched in Henry's memory as a man who did not desert but was deserted on the field. Haunting the boundary lines of traditional war narratives, this spectral figure delineates the extent of what they failed to include. But if Henry's guilt originates from this shadowy figure, it will not, as General McClurg correctly intuits, facilitate his reentry into a conventional ideological framework. Motivated as it is by the specter of the tattered soldier unrepresented by any narrative convention, Henry's guilt does not reactivate representations guaranteed by shame and fear, but acts out the inability of those representations to reabsorb him into the world.

As we have seen, Crane set out to reduce the Civil War narrative to its barest essentials. He stripped the names from the war battles and emptied out the frame of referents enabling the war to confirm for Americans a sense of their place in the history of nations. By driving a wedge between authorized versions of this war and experiences alien to them, Crane caused a fissure to form in the nation's self-conception, which not even the ideology of union would be sufficient to heal.

The Epic of Consciousness: The Anger of Henry Fleming

Chester L. Wolford

> *The immense poetry of war and the poetry of a work of the imagination*
> *are two different things. In the presence of the violent reality of war,*
> *consciousness takes the place of the imagination. . . . It follows that the poetry*
> *of war . . . constitutes a participating in the heroic.*
>
> WALLACE STEVENS

> *War is a teacher who educates through violence; and he makes men's*
> *characters fit their conditions.*
>
> THUCYDIDES

The Red Badge of Courage establishes Stephen Crane as a writer formally and solidly within the great tradition established and fostered by Homer, Virgil, Milton, and others. While including many of the trappings and conventions and much machinery of formal epic, *The Red Badge* also shares with the epic a more essential quality: the tradition of epic competition. Although greatly oversimplified, a broad review of that tradition would read rather like a social history of Western society over the last twenty-five hundred years.

Because it began traditionally with Homer and historically sometime before 400 B.C. in the eastern Mediterranean, the tradition of epic competition is as old as any in Western literature. One version of an ancient romantic work called "The Contest of Homer and Hesiod," for example, relates how Homer and Hesiod competed to determine who was the best poet. A comparison of the recitations,

From *The Anger of Stephen Crane: Fiction and the Epic Tradition.* © 1983 by the University of Nebraska Press.

as well as the judgment of the audience, indicates that Homer was clearly the better of the two. Yet the king of Chalcis in Euboea, where the contest was reportedly held, awarded the prize to Hesiod, saying that "he who called upon men to follow peace and husbandry should have the prize rather than one who dwelt upon war and slaughter."

While demonstrating the antiquity of epic competition, the story makes another point vital to the tradition and to *The Red Badge:* epics and epic poets do not always compete over literary values. Although the reputations of Virgil and Milton as epic poets rest in part upon how well they compare aesthetically with Homer, nonliterary factors such as cultural and religious values also claim the attention of these men. The most important of these values for the epic is the different ideal of heroism held by each poet, particularly regarding the object of man's duty. The Homeric epics may be termed "individual" because they tend to glorify the individual man. Virgil's is a "group" epic because it glorifies Rome and defines the state as a more worthy object of duty than the individual. Milton attempts, among other things, to glorify a Puritan God and to justify worthiness in his sight as the object of man's duty. To the degree that Milton saw man's task as an attempt to reproduce God's kingdom in the self and community of Christians, *Paradise Lost* and *Paradise Regained* become "group" epics. One way, then, to look at the history of the West is as a movement from man being accountable only for himself—man as individualistic and egocentric—to man as part of something larger, more enduring and significant than himself.

Each of these views finds an embodiment in a great epic poet's notion of heroism, for heroism consists of fulfilling the demands of duty. The Homeric hero ascribes to the code of *areté* which demands that he strive ceaselessly for the first prize. The driving force behind all the hero's actions, *areté* often connotes values different from Roman and Christian virtue. Virtues lauded over the last fifteen hundred years and more—loyalty, honesty, charity, fair play—are simply not part of the code of *areté*; Achilles deserted the field and his friends and spent much of the war in an adolescent funk and Odysseus was a liar and a cheat, but both were great warriors and so have the highest *areté*.

What distinguishes Virgil's Aeneas from Homeric heroes is not the greatness of his deeds but the reasons for performing them. Virgil's epithet for Aeneas is *pius,* a term denoting more than "pious" for Aeneas is also "dutiful." Careful to pour appropriate libations for the gods, Aeneas also is concerned for his family and his destiny. Seeker of peace, invincible in war, believer in law, Aeneas is the heroic ideal of the *Romanum Imperium* of Augustus.

To explain how Aeneas, a second-level Homeric hero in the *Iliad,* became a metaphor for Rome in the *Aeneid* would require several volumes of social, intellectual, and literary history that would carry one from Attic to Roman civilizations. The problem for Virgil, however, was that Homer still dominated the genre in Augustan Rome and his heroes were still revered. As a result, Virgil was forced to compete unevenly with Homer. If Rome were superior to Homeric Greece, then the great Roman epic would have to be superior to the Homeric epics. Virgil succeeded, at least politically, by elevating the Roman hero and debasing the Homeric, elevating *pietas* and *areté*. Thus Turnus, *alius Achilles,* embodies *areté*, and when Aeneas kills him in the poem's final lines, Virgil metaphorically "kills" Achilles, *areté*, and the Homeric epic. Later Christian epic poets such Tasso, Camoens, Dante, and Ariosto also despise *areté*—which they saw as almost identical to *hubris*—and show their contempt by assigning it as a quality belonging to their hero's enemies. Milton's Satan belongs to this type, and in spite of his attractiveness as a Homeric or Shelleyan hero, he is nevertheless a personification of evil. Milton's concept of heroism and duty is as complex as his use of the epic medium, but it is also clear that genuine heroism lies in "true patience and heroic martyrdom." The real Christian hero seeks glory by following the New Testament and dedicates his deeds *ad majoram gloriam Dei.* How one plays the game determines whether one wins or loses.

When Crane includes these notions of heroism and duty in *The Red Badge,* he undertakes a task crucial to writing epics. Because these concepts of heroism and duty are among the most influential in Western history, when Crane denigrates and replaces them, he rewrites, in a very real sense, the cultural history of the west.

INWARD REPUDIATIONS

The first chapter of *The Red Badge* presents heroic ideals in the mind of Henry Fleming, a "youth" inclined by instinct toward *areté* but checked by "religious and secular education" so that he feels himself to be a part of something much larger than himself. Henry is introduced into the story and is immediately engaged in a debate over "some new thoughts that had lately come to him." On the one hand, he sees himself in expressly Homeric terms, with "peoples secure in the shadow of his eagle-eyed prowess." In retrospect, he remembers having "burned several times to enlist. Tales of great movements shook the land. They might not be distinctly Homeric, but there seemed to be much glory in them. He had read of marches, sieges, conflicts, and he had longed to see it all. His busy mind had drawn for him large pictures extravagant in color, lurid with breathless deeds." On the other hand, his mother, the voice of Christian-group ideals, "had discouraged him." Her advice upon his enlistment is the advice of the group: "Don't go a-thinkin' you can lick the hull rebel army at the start, because yeh can't. Yer just one little feller amongst a hull lot of others, and yeh've got to keep quiet an' do what they tell yeh." Contrary to Henry's Grecian mood—he would rather have heard "about returning with his shield or on it" —his mother's relationship to Christianity is everywhere apparent. Her only remark upon hearing of Henry's enlistment is "The Lord's will be done," and when he leaves she says simply, "The Lord'll take keer of us all."

As a surrogate mother, the army too puts a damper on his heated individualism. Before leaving home, "he had felt growing within him the strength to do mighty deeds of arms," but after spending "months of monotonous life in a camp," Henry comes "to regard himself as part of a vast demonstration."

Throughout the first half of *The Red Badge,* the competition between the individualism of Henry's *areté* and the collectivism of *pietas* and "heroic martyrdom" swings between extremes. In his first engagement, Henry seems finally to give in to the standards of the group: "He suddenly lost concern for himself and forgot to look at a menacing fate. He became not a man but a member. He felt that something of which he was a part—a regiment, an army, a cause, or a country— was in crisis. He was welded into a common personality which was dominated by a single desire." Soon, the group becomes more important to him than the causes: "He felt the subtle battle brotherhood more potent even than the cause for which they were fighting. It was a mysterious fraternity."

Much has been made of Henry's joining the subtle brotherhood, but few remember that when the army makes a second charge against the regiment, the mysterious fraternity dissolves under an individuality revived by Henry's sense of self-preservation. He turns tail and runs. Although Achilles has more grace and style, the effect is the same in either case: both Henry and Achilles desert their friends in the field. To say, as many do, that Henry should be damned for his desertion is to speak from an historically narrow perspective; from an Homeric standpoint, one cannot be so quick to judge. In fact, no moral judgments necessarily result from Henry's flight. If Henry can get away with it (he does), if no one finds about it (no one does), and if later he can perform "great deeds"(he does), then that is all that matters. By the end of the sixth chapter, Henry's individualism, his Homeric sense, seems to have won a limited victory—victory because Henry has escaped being subsumed by the group, limited because his sense of shame dogs him throughout the novel.

In the novel's first half the battle for Henry's allegiance to Homeric or Christian-group values occurs in Henry's mind. In the first six chapters, Henry's conflicting feelings need little prodding; in the second six, the action of the novel intensifies, as do attacks on his individualism. In this quarter of the novel, Henry enters the "forest chapel," sees Jim Conklin die in a Christ-like way, and is mentally and verbally assaulted by the "tattered man." Here, too, he receives his "red badge of courage."

It should not be surprising in light of the epic structure that this section of *The Red Badge* is filled with religious imagery. Much critical ink has been spilt in a controversy over whether or not Crane, given his naturalistic bent and nihilist vision, intends Jim Conklin, for example, to represent Christ, or the tattered man to represent the Christian-group ideal; many feel that Crane himself was confused about it and that the novel fails because he fails to resolve the problem. From the standpoint of examining the traditional epic qualities of the book, there is no problem. These chapters mark what ultimately becomes a failure of the Christian-group value system—with two thousand years of indoctrination behind it—to make Henry Fleming return to the fold. It is not Crane's intent to have the reader see things in a religious way, but to see Henry succumb to the pathetic fallacy of Christian-colored glasses.

Arriving at a spot deep in the woods, Henry hears the trees "sing a hymn of twilight. . . . There was a lull in the noises of insects as if they had bowed their beaks and were making a devotional pause. There was silence save for the choruses of trees." Henry now sees things through a "religious half light," and the forest seems to form a "chapel" complete with "arching boughs," "green doors," and a "brown carpet."

When Crane places more emphasis on character and action than upon natural scenes, Christian morality and group ethics are even more strongly merged. Both value systems require humility, love, awe, and admiration for something perceived as greater than and outside of the individual. In chapters six to twelve, the screw is tightened on Henry's conscience, demanding both complete subjection and unqualified support. The first person Henry sees after leaving the forest is the tattered man, who, for Henry, embodies the Christian-group ideal. The tattered man is introduced by a dignified and classical anaphora as if he were the subject of an ancient fable: "There was a tattered man. . . ." This archetypal follower listens to an officer's "lurid tale" with "much humility." Rough as the ragged private looks, his voice is as "gentle as a girl's," and when he speaks it is "timidly." His "pleading" eyes are described in a simile bearing a Christian symbol that could not have escaped Crane; they are "lamblike." With a general "air of apology in his manner," the tattered man is so humble, timid and conventionally feminine that he becomes a caricature of a Christian-group member. Even his physiognomy betrays an overwhelming love for the group. "His homely face was suffused with a light of love for the army which was to him all things powerful and beautiful." Crane here takes standard emotional slither from the rhetoric of nineteenth-century religious writers' descriptions of people saved at camp meetings and attaches it to the army. All of the tattered man's questions are uttered "in a brotherly tone," and his "lean features wore an expression of awe and admiration." In short, he must have been meant to be a caricature, for even his breathing has in it a "humble admiration."

It is also clear that Henry sees Jim Conklin in a "religious half light." Stallman's original reading of Conklin as Christ is fundamentally correct if one understands that it is Henry and not Crane who sees Conklin as Christ. Few figures in American literature have a better claim to the trappings of Christ's Passion than does Jim Conklin. His initials are J. C., he is wounded in the side, he dies on a hill, he is a "devotee of a mad religion," and his death stirs "thoughts of a solemn ceremony." Those who deny that Conklin is a Christ-figure usually do so by pointing out that Conklin is a loud, cracker-crunching, rumormonger. Such evidence is specious, since these qualities are part of Jim only before he became "not a man but a member" by staying on the line during the battle. Some also forget that Crane's intent is to show that Henry sees Conklin in this way, not that Conklin is that way.

One way to place the various episodes of the first half into a perspective of the moral and social competition between Christian-group values and the Homeric ideal of individualism (*areté*) may be to describe that epic competition as a representation of the psychology of Christian conversion from an egocentric individualism to an altruistic membership in the flock. The pattern is similar; as a moral being, man in Christian process moves from the commission of sin to guilt, to alienation, to a desire for expiation, to confession, and finally to redemption. In the end, the process fails to redeem Henry for Christianity, but it does give him a rough time of it, and it organizes the epic competition and psychology of the novel's first half.

Three particular episodes are representative of this psychological movement. The episodes with Mrs. Fleming, Jim Conklin, and the tattered man each appear to bring Henry steadily closer to rejecting his Homeric individuality while ultimately functioning ironically to force his acceptance of *areté*. By the time he is hit on the head and receives his "red badge of courage," Henry has sloughed off the Christian-group concept of heroism. His red badge is, however, not ironical in that he receives it for an act of cowardice; rather it is an outward sign—what the Greeks called *geras*—of his accomplishment in rejecting two thousand years of social and religious indoctrination. An epic feat.

Occurring in the first chapter, the "Mrs. Fleming" episode serves to increase Henry's feelings of sin and guilt over his Homeric sense of selfish individuality which encompasses egoism, insensitivity, and the pursuit of personal glory at all costs—*areté*. The episode opens with Henry in his hut (and *in medias res*) remembering his earlier thoughts about "breathless deeds," his "burning to enlist," and his having "despaired of witnessing a Greeklike struggle."

Mrs. Fleming is a stereotype of the pious, hard-working, long-suffering, farm boy's mother. Her views are Christian-group oriented and come from "deep conviction." Her "ethical motives" are "impregnable." Guilt and remorse over his insensitivity toward his mother work on Henry as he remembers a scene from his leave-taking: "When he had looked back from the gate, he had seen his mother kneeling among the potato parings. Her brown face, up-raised, was stained with tears, and her spare form was quivering." The effect on Henry is predictable: "He bowed his head and went on, feeling suddenly ashamed of his purposes." Significantly, he is not so much ashamed of enlisting as he is of his purposes, his longing for the glory road of individual heroism that scatters the hurt feelings and genuine needs of others along the roadside. Christians would accuse Henry of *hubris;* Augustan Romans would not chide him for enlisting but for having done so without thought to duty and family; Homeric Greeks would have wondered what all the fuss was about, shrugged their shoulders, and remarked that while the action might be a little sad, it was also probably necessary: how else become a hero? Unlike Homeric heroes, however, Henry leaves for war carrying in his soul the cultural burdens of twenty centuries of self-condemnation for succumbing to *areté*.

It is important to emphasize the universal qualities of the novel in general and of Henry Fleming in particular. He is at once common and uncommon; he is Man rebelling against his Mother, Mankind (or at least the archetypal American in the archetypal American novel) attempting to slough off the past. In the American experience this last action ties Henry closely to the transcendental movement, as well as to such archetypal figures as Huck Finn, Natty Bumppo, Rip Van Winkle, and a host of other American heroes. The difference is that unlike Twain, Cooper, and Irving, Crane is using the formal epic ironically to destroy the tradition of heroism, and epic competition is used because its very purpose is to disparage what the past has considered to be the highest expression of man's duty, courage.

The Jim Conklin episode carries Henry a step further in the process by adding to sin and guilt the anguish of alienation and the desire for expiation through good works. After deserting the regiment and wandering through the forest, Henry joins a band of wounded men moving toward the rear. These men have stood their ground—for God and country possibly, for the group certainly. Their wounds seem to symbolize their sacrifices and their devotion to duty. Seeing them this way, Henry feels alienated: "At times he regarded the wounded soldiers in an envious way. . . . He wished that he, too, had a wound, a red badge of courage." Such a badge would grant to Henry membership and acceptance in the group, would assuage his guilt and close the gap between himself and the others caused by his alienation. Henry's anguish is now greater than during the earlier episode: "He felt his shame could be viewed. He was continually casting sidelong glances to see if the men were contemplating the letters of guilt he felt burned in his brow." At this stage Henry is Stephen Crane's Dimmesdale, and the only difference between the two is that Crane's character ultimately is able to "put the sin at a distance." Hawthorne's protagonist never can.

Feeling that he bears the Mark of the Beast, Henry is then confronted by Jim Conklin's wounds, and in his already anguished state, Henry is quite ready to see in Jim an exceptional Christian devotion to duty and sacrifice for the group. Jim's actions, however, deny Henry expiation and even serve further to heighten his anxiety. Henry's attempts to receive absolution are repulsed, for Jim only wants to be left alone to die: "The youth put forth anxious arms to assist him, but the tall soldier went firmly on as if propelled. . . . The youth had reached an anguish where the sobs scorched him. He strove to express his loyalty. . . . The youth wished his friend to lean upon him, but the other always shook his head and strangely protested. 'No—no—no—leave me be—leave me be— ' . . . . and all the youth's offers he brushed aside." Henry's view of Jim as a Christ is Henry's alone. The youth's attempts to assuage his guilt in a bath of atonement fail; although he asks, he does not receive—Jim Conklin will have none of it. All that remains is Henry's very real and painful desire for redemption. Redemption itself is as far away as ever.

Henry's Christian-group consciousness is pushed to its limits in the "tattered man" episode. There are two "sins" here: one is Henry's refusal to confess his earlier desertion of the regiment, and the other is his desertion of the tattered man, an act which redoubles his guilt. When Henry meets the tattered man, the latter repeatedly asks him, "Where yeh hit?" This question, asked over and over again, causes Henry to feel the "letters of guilt" burned, Dimmesdale-like, into his forehead. Instead of causing Henry to repent, however, the letters merely force him to desert the wounded tattered man and leave him to wander off into the fields to die. Immediately after deserting the tattered man, Henry's guilt reaches almost unbearable proportions: "The simple questions of the tattered man had been knife thrusts to him. They asserted a society that probes pitilessly at secrets until all is apparent. . . . He could not keep his crime concealed in his bosom. . . . He admitted that he could not defend himself." Believing that "he envied those men whose bodies lay strewn" on the field, he explicitly wants to be redeemed: "A moral vindication was regarded by the youth as a very important thing."

Confused, guilt-ridden, and afraid that the group may discover his "sin," Henry's mind goes through, as in the first chapter, the same metronomic movement between the demands of the group and the desires of the individual, but with more pain. Henry's anguish remains severe throughout the eleventh chapter. In the twelfth chapter, however, this changes.

Chapter 12 is the last chapter of the first half of *The Red Badge.* Like the end of the first half of the *Iliad,* the *Odyssey,* the *Aeneid, Paradise Lost,* and other epics, it includes both a culmination of the first half and a preparation for the second. In the twelfth book of the *Iliad,* the

Trojans have broken into the Greek encampment. They are never again so close to victory. In the *Odyssey*, the hero nears the end of his wanderings and sets off in the next book for a final successful junket to Ithaca, where he will lay plans to set his house in order. In the *Aeneid*, Aeneas is about to land in Italy, thus putting himself in a position to fulfill his destiny by founding the Roman nation. In *Paradise Lost*, the battle in Heaven ends; Satan and his angels have fallen into Hell, and the stage is set for the second half: the fall of man. Similarly, in *The Red Badge*, Henry completes his epic of return by sloughing off his Christian-group conscience: he accepts his individuality, and he is then prepared to battle the group in the second half.

Henry is "reborn" after being hit on the head in chapter 12. The language of the episode is carefully, even poetically, rendered to represent rebirth. After watching a group of retreating soldiers, Henry runs down from a rise, grabs one of the soldiers, and is clouted for his trouble:

> [The other soldier] adroitly and fiercely swung his rifle. It crushed upon the youth's head. The man ran on.
>
> The youth's fingers had turned to paste upon the other's arm. The energy was smitten from his muscles. He saw the flaming wings of lightning flash before his vision. There was a deafening rumble of thunder within his head.
>
> Suddenly his legs seemed to die. He sank writhing to the ground. He tried to arise. In his efforts against the numbing pain he was like a man wrestling with a creature of the air.
>
> There was a sinister struggle.
>
> Sometimes he would achieve a position half erect, battle with the air for a moment, and then fall again, grabbing at the grass. His face was of a clammy pallor. Deep groans were wrenched from him.
>
> At last, with a twisting movement, he got upon his hands and knees, and from thence, like a babe trying to walk, to his feet. . . . he went lurching over the grass.
>
> He fought an intense battle with his body. His dulled senses wished him to swoon and he opposed them stubbornly, his mind portraying unknown dangers and mutilations if he should fall upon the field. He went tall soldier fashion.

Structurally, the passage focuses first on the falling away of the old in a metaphorical death. Henry loses his sight, his hearing, and then his ability to stand erect. In the middle is a five-word, one-sentence paragraph describing a "sinister struggle" between life and death. From there, the reborn Henry gets up on his hands and knees "like a babe," and finally is able to walk. In spite of the almost allegorical nature of the passage, its essence remains one of a very physical, almost literal, and, most important, quite individual rebirth.

One cannot help but think that the anthropological cast of the passage is intentional. At least, it demonstrates that Crane, however unconsciously, was aware of the consequences for thought of the Darwinian revolution. For Henry, as for mankind, the traditional past could no longer provide solace. Indeed, as the second half of *The Red Badge* shows, the traditional past had to be rolled up and replaced by naturalism and impressionism. These terms, given Holton's appraisal of elements shared by definitions of the former and Nagel's definition of impressionism, can be seen in some light as nearly synonymous and as twin effects of *Origin of the Species* and of the dissemination of other scientific discoveries.

The action reported in this passage is unlike anything else in the book. Except for a later instance when he pushes another fellow, it is Henry's only hostile physical encounter in the novel. Certainly this is not Christian-group combat; it is especially unusual for those engaged in modern warfare. Prior to this point all battles have been described as remote from the individual. Cannons roar at each other, and men shoot at "vague forms" shifting and running through the smoke of many rifles. Always the action has been described in terms of one group charging toward or retreating from another. Moreover, his adversary fights under the same flag as Henry.

Here, for the first time, is a representation of a "Greeklike struggle" that once had been merely a part of Henry's dreams. It has not developed as Henry had expected, and may not be distinctly Homeric, but it is close to primitive hand-to-hand combat, and bears little resemblance to the "mighty blue machine" of the group. For the first time, Henry struggles with another man. Further, Henry's wound is unusual for participants in a modern, group war. Henry's wound is not from a bullet, but from the butt end of a modern weapon used as the most ancient of weapons; as one fellow observes, "It's raised a queer lump as if some feller lammed yeh on the head with a club."

Henry's wandering off "tall soldier fashion" after receiving the blow on the head does not mean that Henry has been converted to a group view of things. To see Jim as a Christian-group figure is to make the same mistake Henry made. Strip away the dramatic symbolism of Henry's former vision of Conklin and one is left with a man dying, alone, unwilling to be helped, and as afraid of mutilation as any Homeric hero. Speech and action are "real"; Henry's interpretation of them may not be. When Henry thus goes "tall soldier fashion," it is not necessarily as a Christ-figure. Henry is in no shape at this point to interpret events; in this instance, the information comes directly from the narrator. The dying Jim Conklin and the wounded Henry Fleming are linked, or seem to be linked, only by a desire to escape the group.

Wandering in the gathering darkness, Henry is finally given direction by an epic guide. Like the role of the captain in "The Reluctant Voyagers," the function of the "cheery man" is traditional to the machinery of epic. As Ariadne helps Theseus, Thetis comforts Achilles, Athena aids Odysseus, Venus supports and guides Aeneas, and Virgil leads Dante, so the cheery man helps Henry to gain self-control, and, as Gibson points out, places him in position to confront those forces which he otherwise would have little power to oppose but which he must overcome in order to complete his epic task. The cheery man leads Henry back to the regiment.

Unlike the two men in "The Reluctant Voyagers," Henry appreciates, albeit somewhat after the fact, the cheery man's help. And well he should, for as he staggers towards the campfires of his regiment in the beginning of the second half of *The Red Badge,* he has nearly done the impossible. In a sense, he has performed more courageously than Achilles. Peliades had only to reach his goal of *areté*, while Fleming had first to throw off his sense of sin and alienation. On one level, he has suffered all the slings and "arrows of scorn" that can be shot at an individual by the archers of conscience, guilt, and alienation from the group. On another level, Henry has forced his way back through two millennia of nationalism and Christianity. Such an act is impossible for an ordinary man. To oppose and overcome, even to a limited degree, the teachings of secular and religious culture is an almost incredible, even epic, feat.

OUTWARD WARS

Yet the battle is only half won. As the first twelve chapters are concerned with Henry's struggle to gain individuality of mind, the second half of *The Red Badge* concerns Henry's conflict with the same forces in the externalized, "outside" world. In terms of the epic of consciousness, the first half concerns Henry's escape from the cave, his coming to consciousness, and his gaining self-control, that is, coming to terms with alienation from the other—the group and the rest of the material world—and the fact of death. Having come to terms internally in the first half, he is ready to confront the other externally in the second half. Here, as in the Aeneid, the hero is confronted with a competition between his newfound values and an externalized embodiment and proponent of the value system he has recently overcome internally. In the second half of the *Aeneid*, Aeneas must confront, battle, and finally defeat the Roman version of the Homeric ideal of *areté* embodied in Turnus. In the last half of *The Red Badge*, Henry must confront, engage, and overcome Wilson, who has not only been "converted" and initiated into the group, but also has become the embodiment of Christian-group consciousness and its value system.

When Henry returns to confront the group, to enter into the midst of the "subtle brotherhood," he manages to resist its attempts to "initiate" him into membership. Henry seems aware at this point of the nature of this confrontation, because "there was a sudden sinking of his forces. He thought he must hasten to produce his tale to protect him from the missiles already at the lips of his redoubtable comrades." The "information" is a baldfaced lie: "Yes, yes. I've—I've had an awful time. I've been all over. Way over on the right. . . . I got separated from the regiment. Over on the right, I got shot. In the head. I never saw such fighting." The lie works, and Henry seems to become the lost sheep returned to the fold.

Wilson, the sentinel who recognizes Henry staggering into camp, seems remarkably changed. Henry now views Wilson much as he had viewed the tattered man, only with colder eyes. In the first chapter, Wilson acted the part of a *miles gloriosus*, a parody of Achilles. In that chapter, which mirrors the first book of the *Iliad*, Wilson engaged Jim Conklin in an argument. Like Achilles and Agamemnon, "they came near to fighting over" their differences. Wilson also spent much time bragging about his prowess in battle. Now, however, Wilson seems to embody Christian-group values. When first seen in chapter 13, he is standing guard over the regiment. Upon recognizing Henry, he lowers his rifle and welcomes the youth back: "There was husky emotion in his voice." Later, while dressing Henry's wound, Wilson acts out the feminine role of the soothing and clucking mother hen who welcomes one of her lost chicks back to the coop: "He had the bustling ways of an amateur nurse. He fussed around." When Wilson puts his cloth on Henry's head, it feels to the youth "like a tender woman's hand."

Because he didn't run, Wilson was subsumed by that "regiment, army, cause," or country; he joined the "subtle brotherhood," the "mysterious fraternity born of the smoke and danger of death." At the beginning of the battle neither Henry nor Wilson had gained a genuine sense of individuality; both at that point were vulnerable to the group. Because he ran, Henry was excluded from the ego-annihilating forces which Wilson joined.

As a result, Henry and Wilson are now two very different kinds of men. Wilson, who had earlier jumped at any chance to get into an argument or a fight, now stops a fight between two men; he explains to Henry, "I hate t' see th' boys fightin' 'mong themselves." Henry, however, feels no such obligation to become a peacemaker; he laughs and reminds Wilson of an earlier fight the formerly loud soldier had had with "that Irish feller." Certain that he would be killed, Wilson had given Henry a packet of letters before the first battle with instructions that they be sent home after his "imminent" death. The contrast between Wilson's new-found humility and Henry's arrogance appears when Wilson asks for the letters back. Wilson flushes and fidgets, "suffering great shame." When Henry gives them back, he tries "to invent a remarkable comment upon the affair. He could conjure up nothing of sufficient point. He was compelled to allow his friend to escape unmolested with his packet. And for this he took unto himself considerable credit. It was a generous thing. . . . The youth felt his heart grow more strong and stout. He had never been compelled to blush in such a manner for his acts; he was an individual of extraordinary virtues." There is a double irony here. On one level, the passage mocks Henry, but on another, Henry is essentially correct. He has not been "compelled" to undergo the humility of confession. He has overcome in large measure the need for communal redemption of guilt and shame. He does, indeed, have extraordinary "virtues," but they are the "virtues" of *areté*, pride, and individualism.

As they begin the second day of battle, Henry and Wilson are very soon recognized by the group as entirely different kinds of heroes. First, Henry is transfigured by *menos,* the animal-like battle-rage of Homeric heroes: "Once, he, in his intent hate, was almost alone and was firing when all those near him ceased. He was so engrossed in his occupation that he was not aware of a lull." One man derides him for not stopping when the others had, but the lieutenant (whose "voice" had been described as expressing a "divinity") praises Henry in animistic terms. "By heavens, if I had ten thousand wild-cats like you I could tear th' stomach outa this war in less'n a week." Finally, Henry receives the recognition from the group that Homeric heroes seek. He is viewed a someone separate, distinct, and most important, superior: "They now looked upon him as a war-devil," they are "awe-struck."

Wilson is a hero of a different age. Henry does not incite the group to action; his only concern is for his own heroism. Wilson, the hero of the group, serves this purpose: "The friend of the youth aroused. Lurching suddenly forward and dropping to his knees, he fired an angry shot at the persistent woods. This action awakened the men. They huddled no more like sheep. . . . they began to move forward."

Wilson has become the leader of his flock, and Henry has become a Homeric "war devil."

There are a number of confrontations between Henry and Wilson in their respective roles as individual and group heroes. The morning after Henry's return to camp, for example, Wilson "tinkers" with the bandage on Henry's head, trying to keep it from slipping. Friendly, consoling, and helpful, Wilson is berated by an unfriendly, arrogant Henry: "Gosh-dern it'. . . . you're the hangdest man I ever saw! You wear muffs on your hands. Why in good thunderation can't you be more easy? . . . Now, go slow, an' don't act as if you was nailing down carpet." Henry seems already to have gained superiority over his counterpart: "He glared with insolent command at his friend."

Later, when Henry remembers the letters Wilson had given him, he again feels his superiority and thinks in terms of dominance: "He had been possessed of much fear of his friend, for he saw how easily questionings could make holes in his feelings. . . . He now rejoiced in the possession of a small weapon with which he could prostrate his comrade at the first signs of cross-examination. He was master." Wilson remains a symbol to Henry of Christian-group conscience throughout the second half, and Henry never completely overcomes his own Christian-group sense. It dogs him.

The crucial confrontation between the two heroes is a face-to-face physical encounter on the battlefield. It occurs, fittingly, in a contest to determine who will carry the flag across the field in the charge. For Wilson, the traditional approach to the flag as a symbol of a group is most appropriate. Possession of the flag would mean that Wilson had reached the goal of all group epic heroes: to become the idealized symbol of the group. For Henry, the flag is also a symbol of the group. But Homeric heroes strive after *geras,* the prize, the symbol by which they are acknowledged by the group as superior. Possession of the flag would mean that he had fulfilled the aspect of *areté* that demands that he achieve supremacy over the group. Consequently, the flag becomes for Henry "a goddess, radiant, that bent its form with an imperious gesture to him. It was a woman . . . that called to him with the voice of his hopes."

Since the flag is a symbol both for the group and for the superior individual, it is natural, when the bearer is shot, that both Henry and Wilson should go after the flag. It is also inevitable, although slightly contrived, that they should reach it at the same time: "He [Henry] made a spring and a clutch at the pole. At the same instant, his friend grabbed it from the other side."

Neither Henry nor Wilson relinquishes the flagpole and a "small scuffle" ensues. For Henry, however, possession of the flag means so much in terms of dominance over his peers that he has no compunctions about using force against his comrade: "The youth roughly pushed his friend way."

In gaining the flag, Henry has defeated his Christian-group rival and the value system Wilson champions. Henry has gained supremacy over his peers, achieving his *areté*. Yet the victory is not complete: there is still the enemy's flag. Were Henry to claim that flag as well, he would be proven superior not only to his peers, but also to the collective body. Henry fails. Although there is much heroism in becoming individual, one is never completely freed from the group. Its influences, physical and mental, remain forever. Although Henry has equaled or surpassed the deeds of Achilles and Odysseus, although he has overcome in large measure the long stony sleep of Christian-group culture and heritage, he fails to gain a complete victory. It is as if Henry knows what its possession would mean: "The youth had centered the gaze of his soul upon that other flag. Its possession would be high pride." But Wilson, that champion of the group, had dogged Henry across the battlefield and beat Henry to it by springing like Christ the Panther. "The youth's friend . . . sprang at the flag as a panther at prey. He pulled at it, and wrenching it free, swung up its red brilliancy with a mad cry of exultation."

In terms of the epic tradition, Henry's possessing the other flag could have meant possibly a complete victory for the Homeric epic over the social epic after two thousand years. It might also have meant a winning back of the heroic, individual "soul" after two millennia of suppression by Christian-group value systems, both political and spiritual. But, as the later Scratchy Wilson of "The Bride Comes to

Yellow Sky" and the Swede of "The Blue Hotel" discover, such a victory is fleeting at best and always illusory. Wilson may have lost an individual encounter with Henry, but he has also proven that the group cannot be completely defeated by the individual.

VICTORIES

The epic tradition demands that a writer replace former concepts of epic heroism with his own if he wishes to be more than a mere imitator. In nearly all of Crane's best work, his idea of heroism is his ideal of personal honesty. Repeatedly, Crane measures his characters against this standard; Henry Fleming measures as well as any.

More than any other sort of writer, one whose work has epic dimensions lends to his fictional heroes his own supreme ambition; so much is this so, in fact, that the poet himself may be considered the ultimate hero of his own epic, and is sometimes difficult to separate from the fictional hero. For millennia the epic poet has been set apart from his fellows by his abilities, but especially by the intensity of his vision and by the degree to which he believes in it. For Crane, keeping close to his vision, in terms both of apprehension and of comprehension, is the standard not only of honesty but of heroism as well.

The desire to see clearly runs through *The Red Badge of Courage.* Henry in particular seeks continually to perceive with his own eyes. There are more than two hundred references in *The Red Badge* to Henry seeing, not seeing, or trying to see. However, his sight tends always to be obscured either by the group, which limits what the individual can see, or by a kind of Homeric hero complex in which Henry feels that an individual can see everything. Each is a form of blindness and each corresponds to one of the two epic value systems. There is an implication throughout most of the novel (the implication becomes explicit in the last chapter) that history is little more than an individual interpretation of events raised to a level of cultural reporting and collective interpreting. Both as individual and as representative man, Henry makes his own specific interpretations of events. On the other hand, those interpretations are also colored by epic concepts. If the individual's interpretation is deluded, so is the epic's, and vice-versa.

Since Crane uses "vision" as a metaphor for his own particular notion of heroism, former notions of epic heroism are first debased and then replaced by the use of images and references to seeing. One of the value systems attacked in *The Red Badge* is the Christian-group view, which obscures and distorts the attempts of the individual to "see." The group, in the form of the army or the brigade or the regiment, is constantly associated with smoke or fog. As Henry is about to move into his first engagement, he identifies the fog with the army; indeed, the fog seems to emanate from the group: "The youth thought the damp fog of early morning moved from the rush of a great body of troops." The same image is used in the opening sentence of the novel: "The cold passed reluctantly from the earth, and the retiring fogs revealed an army stretched out on the hills, resting." Smoke is even more often associated with the group. Although realistic in a novel about war before the invention of smokeless powder, the image is used for much more than verisimilitude. At one point the position of an entire brigade is identified only by reference to the position of a blanket of smoke: "A brigade ahead of them went into action with a rending roar. It was as if it had exploded. And, thereafter, it lay stretched in the distance behind a long gray wall that one was obliged to look twice at to make sure that it was smoke." Not only is smoke identified with the brigade, but smoke also seems to give it protection.

The group is also seen in terms of darkness, snakes, and monsters, which in epics and archetypes of the unconscious are usually identified with evil. As the army is forming to march into battle, Henry perceives the group: "From off in the darkness, came the trampling of feet. The youth could occasionally see dark shadows that moved like monsters." As the "monsters" moved off in columns, "there was an occasional flash and glimmer of steel from the backs of all these huge crawling reptiles." And the "two long, thin, black columns" appear "like two serpents crawling from the cavern of the night." The men of the group themselves sometimes appear "satanic" to Henry.

Most often, however, the smoke of the group obscures and distorts Henry's vision. With the smoke of "the war atmosphere" around him in his first engagement, Henry had "a sensation that his eye-balls were about to crack like hot stones." His desire to see is constantly getting in the way of his assimilation into the group, but he can never get an unobstructed view and his other senses are stifled, almost annihilated by the physical and metaphorical "smoke" of the group. Against this smoke Henry directs more of his anger than against a charging enemy: "Buried in the smoke of many rifles his anger was directed not so much against the men he knew were rushing toward him as against the swirling battle phantoms which were choking him, stuffing their smoke robes down his parched throat."

The group has the ability to hide reality from the individual. The group takes away the individual's unobstructed use of his senses—the only means he has of perceiving the world around him. While surrounded by "smoke," a man cannot "see," and will behave in the way the group wants him to behave. Shortly before Henry becomes "not a man but a member," for example, he and the regiment are moving rapidly forward to a "struggle in the smoke": "In this rush they were apparently all deaf and blind."

After he has run, been hit on the head, and returned to the group, Henry sees the regiment in a more sinister aspect. After spending the night in sleep Henry awakes and it seems to him "that he had been asleep for a thousand years." This "sleep," of course, takes him back in time, not forward, and so he sees "gray mists," and around him "men in corpse-like hues" with "limbs . . . pulseless and dead." If every epic hero must visit hell, then, for Henry, being in the middle of the group is just that: he sees "the hall of the forest as a charnel place. He believed for an instant that he was in the house of the dead."

If the group influence which Henry has resisted and over which he has gained some dominance causes the individual to see less than he is able, the Homeric view of man purports to allow the individual to "see" more than he actually can. Crane renders the Homeric view meaningless by showing that it too is clouded. That is, if Wilson, the group hero, is given "new eyes" and now apparently sees himself as a "wee thing," then Henry, the Homeric hero, becomes so caught up in his individual desires that his eyes are reduced to "a glazed vacancy." He becomes a "barbarian, a beast." He sees himself as a "pagan who defends his religion," and he sees his battle-rage as "fine, wild, and, in some ways, easy. He had been a tremendous figure, no doubt. By this struggle he had overcome obstacles which he had admitted to be mountains. They had fallen like paper peaks, and he was now what he called a hero."

The whole of chapter 17 describes Henry as being in the grip of the blind battle-rage of Homeric heroes. He forgets that he is merely a private engaged in a small charge on one day of one battle. He thinks of himself as colossal in size and of the other soldiers as "flies sucking insolently at his blood." Although his neck is "bronzed" and he fires his rifle with a fierce grunt as if he were "dealing a blow of the fist with all his strength," he is essentially what one soldier calls this "war devil": "Yeh infernal fool." Heroic Henry certainly is, even in a traditional way, but a bit foolish as well.

Henry soon gains a truer vision. Going with Wilson to get some water, Henry, as well as his image of himself as a Homeric hero, is deflated by a "jangling general" who refers to Henry's regiment, and implicitly to Henry himself, as a lot of "mule drivers." Henry, who had earlier viewed nature as a sympathetic goddess in language filled with Virgilian pathetic fallacy and Christian symbolism (the forest-chapel, for example), and later as a capricious, sometimes malevolent beast much as Homer saw it, now has "new eyes" and sees himself as "very insignificant." This is not necessarily a Christian sense of insignificance, nor even a completely naturalistic one, but simply a realization that compared with more powerful forces, including the regiment, he is powerless. Moreover, since officers are often associated with gods, the sun, and other natural and supernatural entities, Henry's discovery can be seen as developing from his earlier views of nature.

After discovering his insignificance, Henry is in a position to receive a new heroism, a new vision, a "real" vision. In his charge across the field on the second day of battle, it "seemed to the youth that he saw everything":

> Each blade of the green grass was bold and clear. He thought that he was aware of every change in the thin, transparent vapor that floated idly in sheets. The brown or gray trunks of the trees showed each roughness of their surfaces. And the men of the regiment, with their starting eyes and sweating faces, running madly, or falling, as if thrown headlong, to queer, heaped up corpses—all were comprehended. His mind took a mechanical but firm impression, so that afterward everything was pictured and explained to him, save why he himself was there.

A "mechanical" impression of some blades of grass, tree trunks, and sweating, frightened, dying men: that is all one can ever hope to see. The process of epic has been reversed. Virgil had expanded Homer's view of ten or twenty years of glory on the plains before a small town in Asia Minor to include a long-lived empire encompassing the unknown world. Similarly, the Christian epics of Charlemagne and the crusades are described as world wars. Milton extended the epic beyond human time and farther out than human space. Crane doubled back upon the epic tradition, gradually narrowing space until the epic vision includes only a minute perception and compressing time until that perception exists only for a fleeting instant. It is epical in its achievement and heroic only because Crane has shown it to be the only vision possible for man that remains "bold and clear."

Tiny but unobscured by the smoke of the group or the blinding *menos* of *areté*, Henry's vision has made him Crane's version of the best epic hero. Trying to "observe everything" in his first battle, but failing to "avoid trees and branches," Henry now sees only *something*. Gone is the Roman vision of national destiny and the Miltonic perception of a Puritan God's universe. Heroism is defined in *The Red Badge* as one man's limited but perhaps illusionless vision: grass blades, tree trunks, dying men.

This vision has dominated the literature of the twentieth century and has allowed writers who followed Crane to make the first tentative steps toward a new supreme fiction based upon consciousness of a materialistic universe while discarding the old fictions based upon the imagination. It is upon this vision that Wallace Stevens, for example, built his poetic edifice, and it is because of the new tradition inaugurated by *The Red Badge* that Stevens could write that "in the presence of the violent reality of war, consciousness takes the place of the imagination." That is precisely what happens in this novel.

The epic of consciousness in the *The Red Badge* is clearly set forth. Henry begins the novel in his hut, emblem of the enclosed violence of his mind. In this enclosure, cluttered by cracker boxes, clothing, and utensils, he gives vent to his cluttered and conflicting fears and anxieties. "Convicted by himself of many shameful crimes against the gods of tradition" and feeling "alone in space," he has "visions of a thousand tongued fear," and admits that "he would not be able to cope with this monster." When he first goes into combat, he sees "that it would be impossible for him to escape from the regiment. It enclosed him. And there were iron laws of tradition and laws on four sides. He was in a moving box." After escaping from the regimental enclosure, he enters a succession of archetypes for the unconscious—the forest, a swamp, "deep thickets" —each enclosing those which follow, until he reaches "a place where the high, arching boughs made a chapel." Here is a different sort of cave, for this is not at first the enclosure of unconscious fears, nor an enclosure of transcendence, but rather a false cave, like the den of Error (book 1, canto 1) and the cave of Mammon (book 2, canto 7) in the *Faerie Queene,* where the hero is lured toward a false transcendence. In Henry's case the promise comes in the form of religious transcendentalism. While the insects are praying and the trees are whispering, Henry pushes open the "green doors" and enters the chapel. In a paragraph or two Crane both anticipates W. W. Hudson and Edgar Rice Burroughs and parodies the Schianatulander and chapel scenes of *Parzival,* for Henry has no sooner entered and is standing "near the threshold," when "he stopped horror-stricken at the sight of the thing."

> He was being looked at by a dead man who was seated with his back against a column-like tree. The corpse was dressed in a uniform that once had been blue but now was faded to a melancholy shade of green. The eyes, staring at the youth, had changed to the dull hue to be seen on the side of a dead fish. The mouth was opened. Its red had changed to an appalling yellow. Over the grey skin of the face ran little ants. One was trundling some sort of a bundle along the upper lip.

The stark clarity of this paragraph, with its excruciatingly painful materialism, provides a perfect contrast to the "religious half-light" leading up to this description. While the description is faintly reminiscent of Thoreau's mock epic paragraphs on ants in *Walden,* its main purpose seems to be to pose starkly the problem that Henry and other epic heroes must face. Somehow, the pathetic fallacy, the religious rose-colored glasses, must be removed, and Henry must still be able to face the "thing" —the fact of death. At this early stage, the contrast is too great for Henry and he responds by screaming and fleeing from the enclosure, which promised transcendence but delivered only death. Another way of saying it is that he was lulled by the imagination and then confronted by pure consciousness. He heads back to the regiment. Only later, after facing death in the field, does Henry accept a classical, almost Lucretian materialism with respect to mortality. This seems to be what Henry learns: "He knew that he would no more quail before his guides wherever they should point. He had been to touch the great death and found that, after all, it was but the great death."

Before this, however, Henry has other caves to face. It may be said that after he crosses the river in chapter 3, Henry is subterranean for nearly the remainder of the novel, much as Dante is throughout the *Inferno.* The others are merely caves within caves, hells within Hades. One of these is the night camp of the regiment in chapter 13. Here Henry catches "glimpses of visages that loomed pallid and ghostly, lit with a phosphorescent glow." Another enclosure of failed transcendence, this camp is like that to which the captain brings the reluctant voyagers. This too contains a window on the stars: "Far off to the right, through a window in the forest could be seen a handful of stars." Managing to resist the temptations of even this "charnel house," Henry subsequently overcomes the numerous enclosures form-ed by the smoke of the regiment's many rifles and achieves his "bold and clear" vision.

DEFEATS

The latest episode in the long controversy about the quality of *The Red Badge* begins with Henry Binder's 1978 article and 1979 edi-tion of Crane's novel for *The Norton Anthology of American Literature—* articles in which he proposes restoring, and an edition in which he does restore, several manuscript passages to the printed text. Restor-ing these passages, Binder claims, makes a muddled novel clear and consistent. The controversy regarding whether or not Henry "grows" is resolved: he does not; the novel is clearly ironic. While agreeing that the original Appleton edition poses problems, Donald Pizer contends that the traditional text is the best we have until evidence stronger than Binder's appears. Pizer takes issue with Binder on essentially two points: first, that because there is no evidence suggesting that Crane was pressured into making the cuts, it can only be assumed that he freely chose to make them; and second, that Binder errs in assuming that "a clear and consistent novel is better than an ambivalent and ambiguous one."

Because it involves an entire chapter, the longest of Binder's ad-ditions must be addressed in some detail by anyone discussing the struc-ture of *The Red Badge*. This is especially true of a discussion of classical epic structure, where arithmetical divisions are significant and the notion of a twenty-five-chapter epic poses some problems. The restored chapter is the original manuscript's chapter twelve, coming after the Appleton chapter eleven. Traditional epics are structurally divided in half. A twenty-five-chapter novel based on epic would be divided somewhere near the middle of chapter thirteen, leaving twelve and a half chapters on either side. Chapter thirteen in the new Norton edi-tion is chapter twelve of the traditional Appleton edition. The middle of this chapter describes Henry receiving his wound, a description already discussed as pivotal to the work. Since Henry is in no posi-tion to do much on his own between the time he is wounded (the middle of the Norton) and the time the Cheery man deposits him with the regiment (ending the traditional text's first half), the different editions have little effect on the validity of the novel's epic structure.

The content of the added chapter does little more than reaffirm the metronomic quality of Henry's thoughts and emotions as they move between extremes of Nietzschean egotism and Paulean self-flagellation. On one hand, "it was always clear to the youth that he was entirely different from other men; that his mind had been cast in a unique mold. Hence laws that might be just to ordinary men, were, when applied to him, peculiar and galling outrages." On the other hand, when "his mind pictured the death of Jim Conklin" and in it "he saw the shadows of his fate," he felt himself to be "unfit": "He did not come into the scheme of further life. His tiny part had been played and he must go."

The additions appearing in the 1979 Norton edition of *The Red Badge* do little to enhance or diminish the notion of the *The Red Badge* as having structural and thematic roots in classical epic. At the same time, since the passages do little more than reaffirm the greatness of *The Red Badge,* the classical dicta of economy and simplicity ought to apply, and one giving a supposedly classical reading of a work ought to side with his sources.

The final chapter of *The Red Badge* presents perhaps the greatest critical problem in the Crane canon. Many of the critical reservations about Crane's importance and abilities rest in the complexities and sup-posed inconsistencies (even inanities) of this chapter.

The last chapter is both complete and consistent. It is a deliberate reversal of all that has gone before. Throughout the largest portion of *The Red Badge,* Henry is in the process of sloughing off both the Christian-group "walking-sticks" of Stallman's interpretation and the Homeric "creeds" of this reading. If the final chapter of *The Red Badge* is naturalistic, it is so only within the context of Crane's conception of the epic.

That a man may learn and then forget, as Holton says, pervades Crane's writings; in terms of the epic nature of *The Red Badge,* a man may forget and then remember. In the first twenty-three chapters, Henry proceeds to "forget" all previous cultural notions and epic concepts about the way life is. Having "forgotten," he finally achieves an im-pressionistic vision of the individual man unencumbered by epic and cultural trappings. In the final chapter, however, Henry "remembers"; his former epic value systems sweep back over him, and he is left at the end dreaming dreams he had dreamt in the beginning.

Throughout twenty-three chapters of the novel the major concern is to discover the true nature of heroism. In the final chapter, however, all epic values are specifically refuted. Because he forgets the vision that he has found, and the limited heroism he has discovered, Henry becomes a nonhero. *The Red Badge,* too, is negated, a nonepic. Unlike Milton, Virgil, and Homer, Crane does not wait for his particular notion of heroism to be satirized by others; he mocks it himself.

The Red Badge of Courage ends by mocking the epic and its heroic ideals. But the novel, so saturated with epic tradition, cannot be exiled from the epic province. Its exploitation of epic conventions attests to the lingering vitality of the genre, but its annihilation of heroism—Homeric, Virgilian, Catholic, or Miltonic—at the same time exposes the genre's vulnerability. The novel marks a transition from the formal epic tradition to all that is Homerically nonepic in modern fiction: triumphant chaos and successful deceit.

The last chapter is an ironic recapitulation of each epic value system present in the remainder of the book. Homeric *areté* is savagely mocked, as is Christian-group heroism. The primary target, however, is that final concept of heroism, Crane's own, which Henry has achieved earlier: that concept based only on the individual's ability to peer into the pit of reality with a gaze unclouded by cultural and epic notions of what the world is like. Throughout this final chapter, Henry's (and Crane's) perception-based, impressionistic heroism is mocked by means of an ironic significance attached to images of and references to the sense of sight. Henry enters the chapter a cleareyed hero; he exits blind and deluded.

As the chapter opens, the battle has begun to wane and the sounds of war have begun "to grow intermittent and weaker." Henry's newfound vision soon runs the gamut of perception from egotistical pride to cringing guilt and humility, and is, in effect, also becoming "weaker." As the regiment begins to "retrace its way" like a snake "winding off in the direction of the river," Henry is with it, recrossing the Stygian stream he had crossed in chapter 3. Similarly, Henry's mind is "undergoing a subtle change": "It took moments for it to cast off its battleful ways and resume its accustomed course of thought. Gradually his brain emerged from the clogged clouds and at last he was enabled to more closely comprehend himself and his circumstance." After "his first thoughts were given to rejoicings" because he had "escaped" the battle, Henry's vision becomes distorted. First, he contemplates his "achievements." With Homeric eyes he sees his deeds as "great and shining." His deluded vision is so distorted that he dresses those deeds in the royal "wide purple and gold," which, on Henry, give off sparkles "of various deflections."

Next, he assumes Christian eyes, and his visions of Homeric glory, of *areté*, are destroyed by an exaggerated guilt brought on by the memory of his crime against the tattered man. The tattered man had tormented him unmercifully, but all Henry sees is a grotesquely distorted image of the gentle tattered man transmogrified into a weird Christian version of some apostle of revenge who visits on Henry a "vision of cruelty." One delusion displaces another, so that Henry's previous vision, as well as his heroism, becomes changed and meaningless, because no longer is it his alone. Homeric pride makes Henry a strutting fool, and Christian-group guilt betrays him as a coward.

Images of and references to vision provide further ironic commentary on the quality of "perception" inherent in the two traditional epic value systems. For example, Crane mocks three specific aspects of *areté* in the final chapter by proving them to be false or wildly exaggerated visions of reality. He first mocks the lack of any firm moral sense in the ancient Greek battle code. At times, Henry has done less than his *areté* demands of him, but he rightly ignores this when contemplating his great deeds and he even feels "gleeful and unregretting." Another aspect of *areté* mocked by Crane is the all-important result of the Homeric hero's desire for glory, "public recognition of his *areté*: it runs through Greek life." Henry tends to exaggerate the quality of his *areté*, and consequently the recognition it deserves, in a sort of daydream vision, a "procession of memory" in which "his public deeds were paraded in great and shining prominence." The final mockery concerns that aspect of heroism lying at the heart of *areté*: the recognition of the hero's superiority over his peers. If we remember the soldier's comic, even ridiculous speech concerning "Flem's" bravery and the somewhat qualifying and dubiously conferred title "jimhickery," Henry's recollections seem to be all out of proportion: "He recalled with a thrill of joy the respectful comments of his fellows upon his conduct."

Henry's progression toward heroism during the first twenty-three chapters reverses and inverts itself in the last chapter, for Henry's vision is a distortion that destroys his notion of Homeric bravery and of *areté*. Henry's semi-sin of leaving the tattered man haunts him. Crane here employs a parody of nineteenth-century Protestant tracts, much as he has described Henry's Homeric deeds in the language traditionally used to depict the victory marches of great warriors: "A spectre of reproach came to him. There loomed the dogging memory of the tattered soldier—he who gored by bullets and faint for blood, had fretted concerning an imagined wound in another; he who had loaned his last of strength and intellect for the tall soldier; he who, blind with weariness and pain, had been deserted in the field." Henry is then "followed" by a "vision of cruelty" which clings "near to him always" and darkens "his view of these deeds in purple and gold." This "somber phantom" heightens Henry's guilt; he becomes "afraid it would stand before him all his life." Thus, "he saw his vivid error." After recognizing that he had sinned, Henry receives partial expiation in the form of partial forgetfulness: "Yet he gradually mustered force to put the sin at a distance. And at last his eyes seemed to open to some new ways. He found that he could now look back upon the brass and bombast of his earlier gospels and see them truly. He was gleeful when he discovered that he now despised them." Henry here exchanges one false view of himself for another. The Homeric vision has given way to a Christian-group one. Crane, with beautiful, lyric irony, moves Henry away from the war and from the battle in his mind: "So it came to pass that as he trudged from the place of blood and wrath his soul changed." Henry now believes that "the world was a world for him," as a Christian-group hero should.

There is yet another way, however, in which Crane sets about to destroy the epic. By ironically disparaging the epic view of man's history, Crane ridicules the concept that readers have of the epic genre. The epic has long been one of the more revered forms of historical interpretation and cultural expression. Through epic poetry Homer presents man as a godlike animal struggling to gain a measure of immortality through the public recognition of great deeds. But the Homeric man was like Lear in the storm—alone, naked, and "unaccommodated" —and this is probably why Crane preferred this view more than other traditional views: it was closer to his notion, expressed in "The Blue Hotel," that "conceit is the very engine of life." Virgil gave man more hope by giving him the opportunity to identify and merge with the immortality of a national group. By interpreting history in terms of a great empire, he was also in some measure espousing a kind of immortality. Medieval and Renaissance epic, including *The Song of Roland* and Tasso's *Gerusalemme liberata,* glorified the church militant, ordained to victory. Milton went even farther. He regarded man as completely unworthy of immortality, but acknowledged man's hope in a merciful God's love; man's earthly history spans the interval between creation and final redemption.

Crane felt that these interpretations of history were, to one degree or another, part of a giant hoax willfully perpetuated on man by man. At times he could be downright Aeschylean: "Hope," as Berryman quotes him, "is the most vacuous emotion of mankind."

The Red Badge is a denial of the epic view of history, which Crane felt creates an absurd, illusory, and vacuous emotion.

In the first twenty-three chapters of *The Red Badge* an epic fable is presented which carries the reader back through history. Henry begins *in medias res,* confused and torn between the two major epic views of history, and between two epic value systems as they have filtered through the epic into and out of culture. One of Henry's great accomplishments is his success in throwing off, if only for a short time, the Christian-group view that has dominated the long history of the social epic—indeed of all intellectual life in the West. Next, Henry rejects the rest of history, as recorded by the individual epic, by sloughing off the hope of being an immortal, Homeric "war devil." Finally, past all Christian doctrine, beyond the emotional slither of patriotism and breast-beating brass and bombast, this young man finds a vision in some blades of grass and the grooved bark of a few trees. He is, for an instant, free as few have ever been free; he is loosed from the illusions of history. Perhaps, because it is so limited in duration, Crane is mocking his own illusion, and that of Americans from Franklin to Ginsberg, that man can indeed throw off the process of history and the illusions it etches into the brain.

However, those twenty-three chapters may not be a fairy-tale epic. Crane may have felt that through catalytic and catastrophic experiences like war, man can scrape the scales of history from his eyes. Perhaps all the teachings of history are reduced to absurdity in the midst of the immense experience, if one tries hard enough to see for himself. Perhaps one can universalize Crane's statement that "a man is only responsible for the personal quality of his honesty" of vision. "A man is sure to fail at it," he said, "but there is something in the failure." Although the paucity of the vision may make it ironic, there is some heroism involved in the sheer ability to perceive reality. In either case, however, the last chapter of the novel indicates that Crane felt heroism to be impossible beyond the immediacy of experience.

This aspect of the last chapter functions by way of a metaphorical equation: memory is to the individual as history is to the species. As Henry moves away from the immediate experience, his memory creates lies and delusions about that experience. The ironic laughter from Crane results from his belief that man cannot really learn from experience, even when he can reach an illusionless view of reality through that experience. Once it is over, once one is no longer staring at the face of red death, then memory, or history, distorts that experience all out of any recognizable proportion.

In the last chapter, history becomes what memory becomes—a mechanism for man to build his self-image. Through the two main thrusts of the history of Western civilization, as expressed by the epic genre, man is deluded into believing himself to be either more or less than he actually is. In the end, Henry is led by his memory to believe with conviction all the mad, distorted hopes of epic history. Ironically, "at last his eyes opened on some new ways." These are new ways only for Henry: they are as old as history. Darwin mounted on Mather.

These "new ways" are a collation of Homeric and Christian-group values. There is still much pride in Henry, but also much humility. Together, they form a paradoxically proud humility: "He felt a quiet man-hood, non-assertive but of sturdy and strong blood." The sum of Henry's wisdom, apparently gained from these seemingly "new" ways, and required of epic heroes, is expressed in what becomes, upon close examination, a meaningless platitude worthy of the climax of a dime-novel adventure: "He had been to touch the great death, and found that, after all, it was but the great death. He was a man."

The final delusion of history and memory Crane repudiated is that of "hope." Part of the reason that Virgil and Milton wrote epics was to give men hope. Beautifully parodic, and powerfully ironic, the last paragraphs of *The Red Badge* express the hopes of Aeneas and Adam, of Columbus and Hiawatha, and of people at all times and in all places, hot to cool, hard to soft, pain to pleasure, hell to heaven:

> So it came to pass that as he trudged from the place of blood and wrath, his soul changed. He had come from hot-ploughshares to prospects of clover tranquilly and it was as if hot-ploughshares were not. Scars faded as flowers.
>
> It rained. The procession of weary soldiers became a bedraggled train, despondent and muttering, marching with churning effort, in a trough of liquid brown mud under a low, wretched sky. Yet the youth smiled, for he saw that the world was a world for him though many discovered it to be made of oaths and walking-sticks. . . . The sultry nightmare was in the past. He had been an animal blistered

and sweating in the heat and pain of war. He turned now
with a lover's thirst, to images of tranquil skies, fresh
meadows, cool brooks; an existence of soft and eternal peace.

No one lives a life of "soft and eternal peace," except in deluded dreams,
and Crane knew it. "He was almost illusionless," Berryman said of
Crane, "whether about his subjects or himself. Perhaps his only illusion was the heroic one; and not even this . . . escaped his irony."

Stephen Crane's Upturned Faces

Michael Fried

In a well-known passage early on in *The Red Badge of Courage,* Henry Fleming (whom the narrative mainly refers to as "the youth") encounters the first of several corpses that turn up in the novel:

> Once the line encountered the body of a dead soldier. He lay upon his back staring at the sky. He was dressed in an awkward suit of yellowish brown. The youth could see that the soles of his shoes had been worn to the thinness of writing paper, and from a great rent in one the dead foot projected piteously. And it was as if fate had betrayed the soldier. In death it exposed to his enemies that poverty which in life he had perhaps concealed from his friends.
>
> The ranks opened covertly to avoid the corpse. The invulnerable dead man forced a way for himself. The youth looked keenly at the ashen face. The wind raised the tawny beard. It moved as if a hand were stroking it. He vaguely desired to walk around and around the body and stare; the impulse of the living to try to read in dead eyes the answer to the Question.

All of Stephen Crane's formidable powers of defamiliarization are quietly at work in this passage. The corpse is inert but active, betrayed

This essay as it appears here is the first part of chapter 2 in Michael Fried's forthcoming book, *Realism, Writing, Disfiguration: On Thomas Eakins and Stephen Crane.* © 1987 by The University of Chicago. The University of Chicago Press.

and poverty-stricken but also invulnerable and forcing, avoided by the ranks of living men, which we imagine parting to give it a certain berth, and yet its tawny beard is manipulated by the wind in a gesture of extraordinary intimacy that more than anything else establishes the dead soldier's uncanniness for us. As for Henry Fleming's relation to the corpse, it is at once apparently straightforward, as when we are told that the youth could see the soles of the dead man's shoes or that he looked keenly at the dead man's face, and conspicuously indeterminate, as when Crane's prose formulates thoughts that could not possibly be those of his protagonist ("And it was as if fate had betrayed the soldier.") but seem nevertheless to follow from the latter's perceptions. Indeed the apparent straightforwardness itself has disconcerting aspects. Thus the succession of grammatically simple sentences in the second paragraph ("The youth looked keenly at the ashen face. The wind raised the tawny beard. It moved as if a hand were stroking it.") seems almost to imply causal relationship, as if the youth were acting on the corpse through the medium of the wind, though characteristically the next sentence (beginning "He vaguely desired to walk around and around the body and stare . . .") comes close to dissolving the distinction between living and dead both by virtue of the ambiguity of the initial pronoun and because staring is precisely the action attributed to the corpse in the second sentence of the first paragraph. It is as though throughout the passage the separateness of the youth both from the corpse and from the narrator is palpably the accomplishment of *absolutely* local effects of writing, which here as elsewhere in *The Red Badge* suggests that we may be in the neighborhood of a "sublime" scenario of fantasized aggression, identification, and differentiation not unlike the one that partly governs the painter's relation to key personages in *The Gross Clinic.*

But my aim in citing this passage is not to insist on that affinity. Instead I want to emphasise, first, the salience in both paragraphs of a particular bodily position, that of the corpse lying flat on its back (this is what allows the wind to get at the beard); second, the characterization of the corpse's upward-staring face as an object of another character's keen attention and the related fact that something, in this case something seemingly gentle, is done to the face or at least to a metonym for it (the tawny beard); and third, the dramatization, through the image of the protruding foot, of an unexpected detail— that the soles of the dead soldier's shoes "had been worn to the thinness of writing paper." I won't try to gloss these matters here but will move directly on to another passage in Crane, this one from his novella *The Monster*.

The passage is taken from an astonishing scene in which the Negro Henry Johnson, who works for the Trescott family as a coachman, goes heroically into a burning house in order to save young Jimmie Trescott from certain death. Johnson rushes up the stairs and finds Jimmie having just awakened in his own room, but when he tries to carry the boy down he discovers that flames and smoke have made the route impassable. For a moment he despairs, then recalls a private staircase leading from another bedroom to an apartment that Jimmie's father, a doctor, had fitted up as a laboratory. But when Johnson finally makes his way there he discovers not only that that room too is on fire but that the doctor's chemicals are exploding in fantastic hues and forms ("At the entrance to the laboratory he confronted a strange spectacle. The room was like a garden in the region where might be burning flowers. Flames of violet, crimson, green, blue, orange, and purple were blooming everywhere. There was one blaze that was precisely the hue of a delicate coral. In another place was a mass that lay merely in phosphorescent inaction like a pile of emeralds. But all these marvels were to be seen dimly through clouds of heaving, turning, deadly smoke"). After pausing on the threshold, Johnson rushes across the room with the boy still in his arms; just then an explosion occurs and "a delicate, trembling sapphire shape like a fairy lady" blocks his path; Johnson tries to duck past her but she is "swifter than eagles" and her talons are said to catch in him as he does so. Whereupon, "Johnson lurched forward, twisting this way and that way. He fell on his back. The still form in the blanket flung from his arms, rolled to the edge of the floor and beneath the window." (Jimmie will later be saved.) The scene concludes:

> Johnson had fallen with his head at the base of an old-fashioned desk. There was a row of jars upon the top of this desk. For the most part, they were silent amid this rioting, but there was one which seemed to hold a scintillant and writhing serpent.
>
> Suddenly the glass splintered, and a ruby-red snakelike thing poured its thick length out upon the top of the old desk. It coiled and hesitated, and then began to swim a languorous way down the mahogany slant. At the angle it waved its sizzling molten head to and fro over the closed

eyes of the man beneath it. Then, in a moment, with mystic impulse, it moved again, and the red snake flowed directly down into Johnson's upturned face.

Afterward the trail of this creature seemed to reek, and amid flames and low explosions drops like red-hot jewels pattered softly down it at leisurely intervals.

By the end of this passage we again are presented with an unmoving body lying face up on the ground. In this case the body is not that of a corpse and its eyes are closed rather than open; but the extent of the author's, or say the novella's, investment in the body's final position becomes plain when we consider the oddly unpersuasive account of the lurchings and twistings that produce it. Another difference from the description of the corpse in *The Red Badge* is that no second character is represented gazing at Johnson's upturned face. But the passage from *The Monster* narrates the destruction of Johnson's face (we are soon told that "he now had no face. His face had simply been burned away") and the remainder of the plot will turn on the dreadfulness to sight of the nonface with which he has been left (although never described, it gives rise to horrendous consequences whenever it is glimpsed). Maybe too the sheer gorgeousness of the color imagery of the burning laboratory should be read in part as a displacement of effects of seeing that the logic of the narrative doesn't allow the scene to represent directly (the "sapphire shape like a fairy lady" comes closest to being a possible agent of vision). In any event, something is done to Johnson's face, and this time what is done is far from gentle. Finally, in light of the comparison of the soles of the dead man's shoes to writing paper in the excerpts from *The Red Badge*, I am struck by the fact that Johnson ends up lying "with his head at the base of an old-fashioned desk," a piece of furniture that one inevitably connects with the activity of writing; and just in case this seems to be making too much of an incidental detail, I shall quote again the sentence that immediately precedes the account of Johnson's appalling disfiguration, but with two key verbs italicized: "For the most part, they [the jars on the desk] were silent amid this *rioting,* but there was one which seemed to hold a scintillant and *writhing* serpent." Whether or not we understand the particular jar to contain ink, the verbs in question evoke a third verb, *writing,* that comes close to rhyming, audially and visually, with the other two. (Later in this essay I shall argue that the images of serpents and fire that turn up frequently in

Crane's texts belong essentially to a metaphorics of writing.)

The third text by Crane I want to consider is the late short tale "The Upturned Face"; in effect it takes the motifs and preoccupations I have identified in the passages from *The Red Badge* and *The Monster* and constructs around them a brief, two-part narrative of tremendous force and uncertain significance. What ostensibly is narrated is the burial, under enemy fire, of a dead officer by two fellow officers who had served with him for years. The opening paragraphs read as follows:

> "What will we do now?" said the adjutant, troubled and excited.
>
> "Bury him," said Timothy Lean.
>
> The two officers looked down close to their toes where lay the body of their comrade. The face was chalk-blue; gleaming eyes stared at the sky. Over the two upright figures was a windy sound of bullets, and on the top of the hill, Lean's prostrate company of Spitzbergen infantry was firing measured volleys.

Two men from the company are assigned to dig a grave and Lean and the adjutant proceed to search the corpse's clothes for "things" (as the adjutant puts it). Lean hesitates to touch the first bloodstained button on the dead man's tunic but at last completes the search and rises "with a ghastly face. He had gathered a watch, a whistle, a pipe, a tobacco pouch, a handkerchief, a little case of cards and papers." Meanwhile the bullets keep spitting overhead and the two lower ranks labor at digging the grave; their completion of the task is announced in the following short paragraph:

> The grave was finished. It was not a masterpiece—poor little shallow thing. Lean and the adjutant again looked at each other in a curious silent communication.

The two officers proceed to tumble the dead man into the grave, taking care not to feel his body as they do so; after saying a mangled prayer (based, it would seem, on the service for the dead at sea) they are ready to oversee the covering up of his remains. At this point, the first paragraph of the second part of the narrative, the motif of the upturned face returns with new force:

> One of the aggrieved privates came forward with his shovel. He lifted his first shovel load of earth and for a moment

of inexplicable hesitation it was held poised above this corpse which from its chalk-blue face looked keenly out from the grave. Then the soldier emptied his shovel on—on the feet.

Timothy Lean felt as if tons had been swiftly lifted from off his forehead. He had felt that perhaps the private might empty the shovel on—on the face. It had been emptied on the feet. There was a great point gained there—ha, ha!—the first shovelful had been emptied on the feet. How satisfactory!

Suddenly the man with the shovel is struck by a bullet in the left arm and Lean seizes the shovel and begins to fill the grave himself; as the dirt lands it makes a sound— "plop." The adjutant suggests that it might have been better not to try to bury the body just at that time, but Lean rudely tells him to shut his mouth and persists at his task. The tale concludes:

> Soon there was nothing to be seen but the chalk-blue face. Lean filled the shovel. . . . "Good God," he cried to the adjutant. "Why didn't you turn him somehow when you put him in? This— " Then Lean began to stutter.
>
> The adjutant understood. He was pale to the lips. "Go on, man," he cried, beseechingly, almost in a shout. . . . Lean swung back the shovel; it went forward in a pendulum curve. When the earth landed it made a sound—plop. (ellipses Crane's)

Much of the cumulative effect of "The Upturned Face" has been lost in my summary, but even so several points are clear. First, once more we find at the center of the scene a dead man lying on his back staring upward; in fact, as I have noted, we are presented with such a figure twice over, at the opening of the tale, where it is described as lying at the feet of Lean and the adjutant, and at the beginning of the second part, as the first shovelful of dirt is held suspended above it. Second, the corpse's chalk-blue upturned face is on both occasions the principal object of Lean's and the adjutant's attention, and once again something uncanny and in a strong sense disfiguring happens to that face—in fact entire second part of the tale turns on Lean's repugnance at the prospect of having to cover the dead man's face with dirt. (The exact degree of violence this implies seems to fall somewhere between the scenes from *The Red Badge* and *The Monster.*) And third, although a thematics of writing is no more than hinted at by the recurrent epithet "chalk-blue" and perhaps also by the little case of cards and papers that Lean removes from the dead man, the newly excavated and still empty grave is characterized, indeed is half-addressed, as "not a masterpiece—poor little shallow thing," a phrase that, however ironically, deploys a vocabulary of artistic valuation that one can imagine the author applying (again ironically: Crane seems to have thought especially well of this tale) to "The Upturned Face" itself. I suggest too that the ostensible action of the tale—the digging of a grave, the tumbling of a corpse into its shallow depths, and then the covering of the corpse and specifically its upturned face with shovelfuls of dirt—and the movement of the prose of its telling are meant as nearly as possible to coincide, as if each were ultimately a figure for the other: this is one reason why, for example, the text comes to an end with the quasi-word "plop," which is nothing more or less than the verbal representation of the sound made when the last shovelful of dirt falls on the grave, or if not the very last at any rate the one that covers the chalk-blue face once and for all. That the protagonist's name, Timothy Lean, invites being read as a barely disguised version of the author's reinforces this suggestion, all the more so in that the adjutant remains nameless and the dead man is referred to only once, by Lean, as "old Bill." All this is to read "The Upturned Face" as representing, and in a sense enacting, the writing of "The Upturned Face," which as a general proposition about a literary work is today pretty much standard fare. What is interesting to consider, however, is why this particular text lends itself so fully to such a reading, or to broaden our discussion to include the passage from the *The Red Badge* and *The Monster,* what it means that motifs of an upturned face and the disfiguring of that face are in all three cases conjoined with a thematization or, in "The Upturned Face" itself, a sustained if displaced representation of the act of writing.

Here is a partial answer. Just as in Rembrandt Peale's *Graphics* a primitive ontological difference between the allegedly upright or erect "space" of reality and the horizontal "space" of writing/drawing emerged as problematic for the graphic enterprise, and just as in Eakin's art an analogous difference between the horizonal "space" or writing/drawing and the vertical or upright "space" of painting turned out to play a crucial role with respect both to choice of subject matter and to all that is traditionally comprised under the notion of style, so in the production of these paradigmatic texts by Crane an implicit contrast between the respective "spaces" of reality and of literary representation—of writing (and in a sense, as we shall see, of writing/drawing)—required that a human character, ordinarily upright and so to speak forward-looking, be rendered horizontal and upward-facing so as to match the horizontality and upward-facingness of the blank page on which the action of inscription was taking place. Understood in these terms, Crane's upturned faces are at once synecdoches for the bodies of those characters and singularly concentrated metaphors for the sheets of writing paper that the author had before him, as is spelled out, by means of a displacement from one end of the body to the other, by the surprising description of the worn-down soles of the dead soldier's shoes in the passage from *The Red Badge*. (The displacement is retroactively signaled by the allusion to reading in the last sentence of the second paragraph.)

Thus for example the size and proportions of a human face and that of an ordinary piece of writing paper are roughly comparable. An original coloristic configuration of all three faces, either by death making one ashen and another chalk-blue or simply by Henry Johnson's blackness, may be taken as evoking the special blankness of the as yet unwritten page. (A preparatory blankness is associated with Johnson's face—actually with his facelessness—in a scene in Reifsnyder's barber shop; the crucial passage reads: "As the barber foamed the lather on the cheeks of the engineer he seemed to be thinking heavily. Then suddenly he burst out. 'How would you like to be with no face?' he cried to the assemblage.") And their further disfiguration, by the wind that is said to have raised the soldier's tawny beard (in this context the verb betrays more aggressive connotations than at first declare themselves), by the ruby-red snakelike thing that flows down into the unconscious Johnson's visage, and by the shovelful of dirt that Lean agonizingly deposits on the last visible portion of his dead comrade, defines the enterprise of writing—of inscribing and thereby in effect covering the blank page with text—as an "unnatural" process that undoes but also complements an equally or already "unnatural" state of affairs. (It goes without saying that the text in question is invariably organized in *lines* of writing, a noun that occurs, both in plural and singular form, with surprising frequency in Crane's prose, as for example in the sentence, "Once the line encountered the body of a dead soldier.") In fact one way of glossing the tumbling of the body into the newly dug grave in "The Upturned Face" is an acknowledgment that the upward-facingness of the corpse, hence of the page, is not so much a brute given as a kind of artifact—not precisely the result of conscious choice (Lean and the adjutant don't try to arrange the corpse face up) but by the same token not the issue of inhuman necessity (before a word has been written on it, the blank page tells a story of agency).

What remains obscure, however, is why in the passages we have examined the act of writing is thematized as *violent* disfigurement and, especially in those from *The Monster* and "The Upturned Face," why it is associated with effects of horror and repugnance—as though writing for Crane, like painting for Eakins, were in essential respects an excruciated enterprise. Nor does anything I have said begin to answer the broader question of what it means that figures of the blank page and of the action or process of writing play an important role in three of Crane's greatest works.

Chronology

1871   Stephen Crane is born on November 1 in Newark, New Jersey. He is the youngest child of the Reverend Jonathan Towley Crane, a Methodist minister, and Mary Helen Peck Crane.

1878–82 Reverend Crane moves his family to Port Jervis, New York, where Stephen first attends school. After the Reverend's death in 1880, Stephen's mother moves the family to Asbury Park, New Jersey.

1891   Stephen Crane attends Syracuse University, where he meets Hamlin Garland. He leaves after his first year and moves to New York City. Mary Helen Peck Crane dies.

1892   Crane fails at several newspaper jobs but publishes six "Sullivan County Sketches."

1893–94 *Maggie: A Girl of the Streets* is printed privately. Crane meets W. D. Howells. He begins work on *The Red Badge of Courage, George's Mother,* and a collection of poems.

1895–96 Crane travels to Mexico. The publication of *The Red Badge of Courage* and *The Black Riders* wins him instant fame. He publishes a revision of *Maggie* with *George's Mother.* En route to Cuba, Crane meets Cora Taylor, proprietress of a house of prostitution in Florida.

1897   Crane is shipwrecked off the coast of Florida. He bases "The Open Boat" upon the incident. He travels to Greece with Cora Taylor to cover the Greco-Turkish War. Crane writes "The Monster" and "The Bride Comes to Yellow Sky" and becomes acquainted with Joseph Conrad.

1898   *The Open Boat and Other Tales of Adventure* is published. Crane becomes a correspondent in the Spanish-American War.

1899   Crane publishes *War Is Kind*. He resides with Cora in extravagance at Brede Place in England. He suffers a massive tubercular hemorrhage.

1900   Stephen Crane dies of tuberculosis in Bandweiler, Germany, on June 5. *Whilomville Stories, Great Battles of the World,* and *Last Words* appear posthumously. A novel, *The O'Ruddy,* is completed by Robert Barr.

Contributors

HAROLD BLOOM, Sterling Professor of the Humanities at Yale University, is the author of *The Anxiety of Influence, Poetry and Repression,* and many other volumes of literary criticism. His forthcoming study, *Freud: Transference and Authority,* attempts a full-scale reading of all of Freud's major writings. A MacArthur Prize Fellow, he is general editor of five series of literary criticism published by Chelsea House.

JOHN BERRYMAN is widely recognized as one of the finest recent American poets. His collections of verse include *77 Dream Songs* and *His Toy His Dream His Rest.* He also published a collection of essays, *The Freedom of the Poet,* as well as a biography of Stephen Crane. A novel, *Recovery,* was published posthumously.

DANIEL WEISS was Professor of Literature at San Francisco State University. He is the author of a psychoanalytic study of D. H. Lawrence, *Oedipus in Nottingham,* and of the posthumously collected essays in *The Critic Agonistes.*

NORMAN LAVERS is the author of studies of Jerzy Kozinski and Mark Harris, as well as a book of short stories.

JAMES NAGEL is Professor of English at Northwestern University. He has edited *Vision and Value: A Thematic Introduction to the Short Story,* and a volume of critical essays on *Catch-22.*

HAROLD BEAVER is Reader at the University of Warwick, England. He has edited several editions of American literature and has contributed frequently to the *Times Literary Supplement.*

DONALD PEASE teaches English at Dartmouth College. He is the author of *The Legitimation Crisis in American Literature.*

CHESTER L. WOLFORD is Professor of English at Behrend College. He is the author of *The Anger of Stephen Crane* and *Fiction and the Epic Tradition.*

MICHAEL FRIED is Professor of Humanities and the History of Art at The Johns Hopkins University, where he is also Director of the Humanities Center. He has written books on Morris Louis and painting in the age of Diderot, and is currently working on a study of Coubert.

Bibliography

Ahnebrink, Lars. *The Beginnings of Naturalism in American Fiction: A Study of the Works of Hamlin Garland, Stephen Crane, and Frank Norris.* New York: Russell & Russell, 1961.

Bassan, Maurice, ed. *Stephen Crane: A Collection of Critical Essays.* Englewood Cliffs, N.J. : Prentice-Hall, 1967.

Beer, Thomas. *Stephen Crane: A Study in American Letters.* New York: Knopf, 1923.

Bergon, Frank. *Stephen Crane's Artistry.* New York: Columbia University Press, 1975.

Berryman, John. *Stephen Crane.* New York: Sloane, 1950.

Berthoff, Warner. *The Ferment of Realism.* New York: Free Press, 1965.

Bridgman, Richard. *The Colloquial Style in America.* New York: Oxford University Press, 1966.

Cady, Edwin H. "Howells and Crane: Violence, Decorum, and Reality." In *The Light of Common Day.* Bloomington: Indiana University Press, 1971.

―――. *Stephen Crane.* New York: Twayne, 1962.

―――. "Stephen Crane and the Strenuous Life." *ELH* 28 (1961): 376–82.

Cazemajou, Jean. *Stephen Crane.* Minneapolis: University of Minnesota Press, 1969.

Colvert, James. "The Origins of Stephen Crane's Literary Creed." *University of Texas Studies in English* 34 (1955): 179–88.

―――. *Stephen Crane.* San Diego: Harcourt Brace Jovanovich, 1984.

Dunn, N. E. "The Common Man's *Iliad.*" *Comparative Literature Studies* 21, no. 3 (1984): 270–81.

Ellison, Ralph. "Stephen Crane and the Mainstream of American Fiction." In *Shadow and Act,* 60–75. New York: Random House, 1964.

Franchere, Ruth. *Stephen Crane.* New York: Cromwell, 1961.

Gibson, Donald B. *The Fiction of Stephen Crane.* Carbondale: Southern Illinois University Press, 1968.

Greenfield, Stanley B. "The Unmistakable Stephen Crane." *PMLA* 73 (1958): 562–72.

Gross, Theodore L. and Stanley Wertheim. *Hawthorne, Melville, Stephen Crane: A Critical Bibliography.* New York: Free Press, 1971.

Gullason, Thomas A., ed. *Stephen Crane's Career: Perspectives and Evaluations.* New York: New York University Press, 1972.

Hart, John E. "*The Red Badge of Courage* as Myth and Symbol." *University of Kansas City Review* 19 (1953): 249–56.

Holton, Milne. *Cylinder of Vision: The Fiction and Journalistic Writing of Stephen Crane.* Baton Rouge: Louisiana State University Press, 1972.

Johnson, George W. "Stephen Crane's Metaphor of Decorum." *PMLA* 78 (1963): 250–56.

Katz, Joseph. *The Merrill Checklist of Stephen Crane.* Columbus, Ohio: Merrill, 1969.

————, ed. *Stephen Crane in Transition: Centenary Essays.* DeKalb: Northern Illinois University Press, 1972.

Kazin, Alfred. "American Fin de Siècle." In *On Native Grounds.* New York: Reynal & Hitchcock, 1942.

LaFrance, Marston. *A Reading of Stephen Crane.* Oxford: Clarendon Press, 1971.

Linson, Corwin K. *My Stephen Crane.* Syracuse, N. Y. : Syracuse University Press, 1958.

Miller, Ruth. "Regions of the Snow: The Poetic Style of Stephen Crane." *Bulletin of the New York Public Library* 72 (1968): 328–49.

Modern Fiction Studies 5 (1959). Special Stephen Crane issue.

Nagel, James. *Stephen Crane and Literary Impressionism.* University Park: Pennsylvania State University Press, 1980.

Pritchett, V. S. "Introduction" to *The Red Badge of Courage and Other Stories.* London: World Classics, 1960.

Rahv, Philip. "Fiction and the Criticism of Fiction." *Kenyon Review* 18 (1956): 276–99.

Schneider, Robert W. "Stephen Crane: The Promethean Revolt." In *Five Novelists of the Progressive Era,* 60–111. New York: Columbia University Press, 1965.

Shatterfield, Ben. "From Romance to Reality: The Accomplishment of Private Fleming." *CLA Journal* 24 (1981): 451–64.

Smith, Allen Gardner. "Stephen Crane, Impressionism and William James." *Revue Français d'Etudes Americaines* 8 (1983): 237–48.

Solomon, Eric. *Stephen Crane in England.* Columbus: Ohio State University Press, 1965.

Solomon, M. "Stephen Crane: A Critical Study." *Masses and Mainstream* 9 (1956): 25–42.

Stallman, R. W. *Stephen Crane.* New York: Braziller, 1968.

————. *Stephen Crane: A Critical Bibliography.* Ames: Iowa State University Press, 1972.

Studies in the Novel 10 (1978). Special Stephen Crane issue.

Taylor, Gordon O. "The Laws of Life: Stephen Crane." In *The Passages of Thought.* New York: Oxford University Press, 1969.

Trilling, Lionel. "The Roots of Modern Taste and William Dean Howells." *Adelphi* 1 (1952): 499–516.

Tuttleton, James W. "The Imagery of *The Red Badge of Courage.*" *Modern Fiction Studies* 8 (1962): 410–15.

Weatherford, Richard M., ed. *Stephen Crane: The Critical Heritage.* London: Routledge & Kegan Paul, 1973.

Weiss, Daniel. "*The Red Badge of Courage.*" *Psychoanalytic Review* 52 (1952): 32–52, 130–54.

Wright, Morehead. "The Existential Adventurer and War: Three Case Studies from American Fiction." In *America Thinking about Peace and War,* 100–110. New York: Barnes & Noble, 1978.

Acknowledgments

"The Freedom of the Poet" (originally entitled "Stephen Crane: *The Red Badge of Courage*") by John Berryman from *The Freedom of the Poet* by John Berryman, © 1965 by Basic Books, Inc. Reprinted by permission of Basic Books and Farrar, Straus & Giroux. This essay originally appeared in *The American Novel from James Fenimore Cooper to William Faulkner,* edited by Wallace Stegner.

"Psychology and *The Red Badge of Courage*" (originally entitled *"The Red Badge of Courage"*) by Daniel Weiss from *The Critic Agonistes: Psychology, Myth, and the Art of Fiction* edited by Eric Solomon and Stephen Arkin, © 1985 by the University of Washington Press. Reprinted by permission. This essay originally appeared in *The Psychoanalytic Review* vol. 52, nos. 2 & 3 (summer & fall 1985).

"Order in *The Red Badge of Courage*" by Norman Lavers from *The University Review* 32, no. 4 (June 1966), © 1966 by the Curators of the University of Missouri, Kansas City. Reprinted by permission of the author and *New Letters* (formerly the *University of Kansas City Review).*

"Literary Impressionism" (originally entitled "Narrative Methods: 'The Eyes of the World' ") by James Nagel from *Stephen Crane and Literary Impressionism* by James Nagel, © 1980 by Pennsylvania State University. Reprinted by permission of Pennsylvania State University Press, University Park, Pennsylvania.

"Stephen Crane: The Hero as Victim" by Harold Beaver from *The Yearbook of English Studies* 12 (1982), © 1982 by the Modern Humanities Research Association. Reprinted by permission of the editor and of The Modern Humanities Research Association.

"Fear, Rage, and the Mistrials of Representation in *The Red Badge of Courage*" by Donald Pease from *American Realism: New Essays* edited by Eric J. Sundquist, © 1982 by the Johns Hopkins University Press, Baltimore / London. Reprinted by permission of the publisher.

"The Epic of Consciousness: The Anger of Henry Fleming" (originally entitled "The Anger of Henry Fleming: The Epic of Consciousness and *The Red Badge of*

Courage'') by Chester L. Wolford from *The Anger of Stephen Crane: Fiction and the Epic Tradition* by Chester L. Wolford, © 1983 by the University of Nebraska Press. Reprinted by permission.

"Stephen Crane's Upturned Faces" (originally entitled "Realism, Writing, and Disfiguration in Thomas Eakins's *Gross Clinic*") by Michael Fried from *Realism, Writing, Disfiguration: On Thomas Eakins and Stephen Crane* by Michael Fried, © 1987 by the University of Chicago Press. Reprinted by permission. This essay originally appeared in *Representations* 9 (Winter 1985), © 1985 by the Regents of the University of California. Reprinted by permission of the University of California Press.

Index